Thank You for Buy

First, I'd like to extend a personal and very sinc
Freedom. I'm confident that you'll find the vast array
satisfying and easy to prepare. I hope they become s
in mine.

Like the recipes it contains, this book was lovingly crafted by hand—without the backing of a large publishing house, *or* a large publishing house's budget . As a self-published author, I simply don't have access to the typical marketing channels that would be provided by a conventional publisher (such as book tours, paid advertisements, PR departments, or automatic placement of the book in bookstores).

Instead, as a self-published author, I rely on word of mouth and grassroots marketing to help spread the word about <u>Sweet Freedom</u>. And that's where you can help.

If you like what you find inside these pages, or if you've made some of the recipes and are pleased with the results, I'd love to know (you can send me an email at sweetfreedomcookbook@gmail.com or leave a comment on my blog at http://dietdessertndogs.wordpress.com). *Then, feel free to tell everyone else as well!*

If you'd like to help spread the word about *Sweet Freedom*, please consider any (or all) of the following ways:

- Tell your **friends, family, co-workers, classmates, email networks, book club, bridge club, pediatrician, allergist, yoga class, naturopath, nutritionist, kids' teacher--** anyone who might be interested in owning a copy of their own or having it available to clients or patients, either in a waiting room or for sale.

- Ask your **local bookstore or library** to stock the book. They can both order directly from the publisher (Trafford Publishing, at 1-888-232-4444 or www.trafford.com), *but they won't order the book if no one asks them to!* And even if you already own a copy, you can still ask them to stock it—then others can learn about the book, too. Or ask them to put it on display in the store (who doesn't love dessert?)

- **Blog about it** on your blog, or mention it on your webpage. When I first started blogging almost 2 years ago, I was absolutely astounded by the incredible communities of people who shared information, ideas, suggestions, and true friendship on blogs. It's one of the best ways I know to communicate with others.

- **Write a review on amazon.com, amazon.ca, amazon.uk, etc.** (and be sure to let me know if you do!)

- Post the information on your **Facebook page, MySpace, Twitter**, or other social networking sites.

- **Give the book as a gift.** Consider buying it for friends, family, or colleagues who are **vegan or vegetarian, who wish to eat a healthier diet, who are kosher, who have food allergies (or who have kids with food allergies)**--or anyone else interested in a whole foods, natural diet.

- If you're a media type, **consider a feature newspaper article, radio or TV spot about *Sweet Freedom*.** I'll gladly provide in-person interviews (and samples!) for local Toronto-area media, and phone or email interviews for anyone else. (Oh, but for *you*, **Oprah**, I'll make an exception and drive to Chicago).

- **If you're involved in a professional group, association or conference looking for a recipe demonstration or speaker,** I'm happy to oblige. I've spoken at nutritionists' groups, vegetarian events, women's health expos, kosher groups, and book clubs; have appeared on City TV in Toronto; and have taught cooking classes professionally for years. I'd be happy to come out and share some baking ideas or a recipe demo with your group.

Every gesture helps, and is most welcome! Thanks again for your support. And enjoy the recipes!

--Ricki

Sweet FREEDOM

Desserts You'll Love without Wheat, Eggs, Dairy or Refined Sugar

Ricki Heller

Order this book online at www.trafford.com/08-1121
or email orders@trafford.com

Most Trafford titles are also available at major online book retailers.

The author asserts that the information in this book is true and complete to the best of her knowledge; however, it is intended as reference materials only and not as medical advice or a medical manual. The information provided herein is designed to help you make informed decisions about your health and cooking. It is not intended as a substitute for any treatment that has been prescribed by your doctor or alternative health practitioner. If you have concerns regarding your health, I urge you to seek competent medical help.

Note for Librarians: A cataloguing record for this book is available from Library and Archives Canada at www.collectionscanada.ca/amicus/index-e.html

Printed in Victoria, BC, Canada.

ISBN: 978-1-4251-7693-8

Sweet freedom: desserts you love without wheat, eggs, dairy or refined sugar/ Ricki Heller

Includes index.

1. Allergies and sensitivities. 2. Vegan cookery. 3. Cookery (Natural foods). 4. Baked Goods
5. Kosher cookery.

We at Trafford believe that it is the responsibility of us all, as both individuals and corporations, to make choices that are environmentally and socially sound. You, in turn, are supporting this responsible conduct each time you purchase a Trafford book, or make use of our publishing services. To find out how you are helping, please visit www.trafford.com/responsiblepublishing.html

Our mission is to efficiently provide the world's finest, most comprehensive book publishing service, enabling every author to experience success. To find out how to publish your book, your way, and have it available worldwide, visit us online at www.trafford.com/10510

www.trafford.com

North America & international
toll-free: 1 888 232 4444 (USA & Canada)
phone: 250 383 6864 ♦ fax: 250 383 6804
email: info@trafford.com

The United Kingdom & Europe
phone: +44 (0)1865 487 395 ♦ local rate: 0845 230 9601
facsimile: +44 (0)1865 481 507 ♦ email: info.uk@trafford.com

10 9 8 7 6 5 4 3 2

What Customers have said about
SWEET FREEDOM'S recipes:

"I confess, I have a sweet tooth and I was skeptical about how the baking would taste. I couldn't imagine cinnamon buns, brownies and muffins that did NOT contain refined sugar, wheat, dairy products and eggs. I mean, what other ingredients do you use when baking? But the family was more than suitably impressed (including a 16-year old who has a sweeter tooth than I have!). It was all yummy!"

--Paul Lima, Toronto, Ontario

"My family and I just tried your brownies, and we all loved them! But the real test was my 17 year-old son. When I told him they were 'healthy,' he was reluctant, to say the least. To him, 'healthy' means tasteless and unappealing. But after one bite, I couldn't get him to stop eating them! He couldn't believe how delicious they were, or how chocolatey and fudgy. Now he wants to eat [Sweet Freedom] brownies on a full-time basis!"

--Angie Scott-Azouz, Dallas, Texas

"Everything was a huge hit. . . the kids liked your brownies better than the birthday cake I had bought for the party!"

--Paula Tarantino, Woodbridge, Ontario

"I am not a baker by nature but your chocolate chip cookies and coconut macaroons were a breeze. I brought them to a birthday party and kept a few back for the parents. They were a hit with the kids and three mums asked me for the recipe on the spot! They could not believe the list of healthy ingredients. I can't wait to give the frosted cupcakes a try. Bring on the next birthday party!"

--Alison McHugh, Oxford, England

"Everyone could not stop talking about your cake. Your Bundt cake was the talk of the night. It was delicious. The other one was great too. Many thanks and you will be hearing from me in the future."

--Donette Peterkin, Maple, Ontario

"Just wanted to let you know that I loved the Chocolate Chip Blondies. My husband had one of the Chocolate Mint Chocolate Chip Cookies and he loved it too, he said it reminded him of a Chips Ahoy Peppermint Chocolate Chip cookie (except of course your cookies are actually healthy). "

--Jennifer Fernandes, Woodbridge, Ontario

❧ In memory of my mother, and our shared time in the kitchen. ❦

Table of Contents

Acknowledgements

If I truly thanked *everyone* who has had a hand in shaping this book, this section would certainly be longer than any other. From the outset, I've been lucky enough to receive helpful advice, suggestions and encouragement from many individuals. Specifically, thanks go out to the following people:

To everyone who provided inspiration and encouragement through your patronage of Ricki's Kitchen and Bake It Healthy, thank you. To those who attended my cooking classes, to those who bought Bake It Healthy treats at stores and organic markets, to those who provided feedback and ideas for recipes, I am deeply grateful. Thanks in particular to **Sharon at Ambrosia Natural Foods**, who was the first to stock my products in her store, and who was a great champion of Bake It Healthy.

To the many role models and mentors I've known while dreaming up and completing this book (some of whom were not even aware of this role), and others who provided invaluable information: to **Ellen Abraham**, for writing *Simple Treats*, a book that I adore and which provided the initial kernel of so many of these desserts, based on the idea that *yes, you can create delicious, healthy desserts without refined sugar or wheat*; to **Nava Atlas**, for her warm encouragement, feedback and support, and for putting me in touch with so many helpful contacts; to **Dreena Burton**, for her generous response to my initial query, and for dispensing invaluable advice and support to a virtual stranger; to **Amy Clay**, for her good natured and reliable information and contacts; to **Nettie Cronish** for her sage and practical advice, and for sharing her own experiences; to **Caroline Dupont** for setting an admirable example and for providing ideas and publishing information; to **Alisa Fleming**, for her willingness to talk about her own experience and for her enthusiastic cheerleading; to **Lindsay Nixon**, for her generosity in providing a wealth of knowledge, information, and resources; to **jae steele** for sharing her own experience and for providing a wonderful role model and some original marketing ideas; and to **Celine Steen** for her bountiful creativity, empathy and key contact information—thank you all!

To friends and family who've provided support, encouragement and feedback throughout this process, and who tasted countless variations of desserts in the book, thanks go out to **Angie Azouz, Brian Bell, Rosalyn Benatar, Ela Borenstein, Judith Carson, Rosemary FitzGerald, Carla Flamer, Robin Flamer, Barbara Freeman, Martha Greenfield, Barbara Heller, Shari Heller, Raisa Jari, Bev Kravitz, Jan Ravens, Deborah Salsberg, Ali Shefler, Michelle Spring, Eva Tihanyi, Bev Verstege** and **Mark Zeidenberg.** You guys are *the best!*

To the amazing team of recipe testers who baked the treats in their own kitchens and provided feedback, suggestions, variations, and other invaluable support, you are a special bunch indeed, and it was my greatest pleasure working with you. Heartfelt thanks go out to **Morgyn Benstead, Courtney Blair, Liz Clancy, Katy Dacanay, Cheryl Harris, Amanda Levin, Diann Mayer, Ashley McNeill, Jenni Mischel, Shelly Mocquet-McDonald** and **Michelle Spring—** thank you all, so much, for your hard work and incredible devotion to this project.

And **to all the other recipe "testers" out there, the readers who try out the recipes on my blog,** Diet, Dessert and Dogs, I am immensely grateful. It's difficult to describe just how profoundly blogging has changed my life, and how much I appreciate the support and dedication of readers whose regular comments, feedback, and encouragement helped keep me motivated throughout the process. I cannot thank you all enough for reading, for returning regularly, and for letting your presence be known!

To those who helped shape the content and appearance of the book: thanks to **Susan Baker** for your thoughtful and detailed review of Chapter Two; to **Chuck Lidstone,** Electronics Guru, for your incomparable skills and meticulous attention to layout and design; and to **Jenni Mischel,** for your keen eye, skilled editing, and always felicitous suggestions for alternative wordings.

To Cameron (aka "The HH"), thank you for your unwavering support, for sacrificing your weekends and evenings to this project, for your incredibly talented cover work, and (of course) for walking the dogs when I wasn't there.

And finally, **to Elsie and Chaser**, thanks for selflessly helping to dispose of all the leftovers.

What the Symbols Mean

The following symbols are used to indicate which food allergens are absent from each recipe. In some cases, a recipe may offer variations, one of which relates to the symbol (for instance, a recipe may be designated "soy free" even if soy is in the recipe list, as long as an alternative to the soy is listed as well).

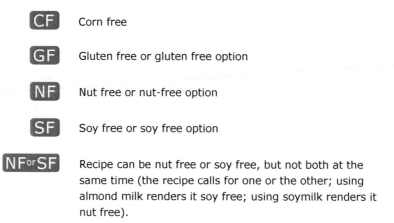

CF   Corn free

GF   Gluten free or gluten free option

NF   Nut free or nut-free option

SF   Soy free or soy free option

NF or SF   Recipe can be nut free or soy free, but not both at the same time (the recipe calls for one or the other; using almond milk renders it soy free; using soymilk renders it nut free).

Please note: these symbols only apply if you've ensured that other ingredients used are free of offending substances as well (for instance, **GF** recipes assume you're using gluten-free baking powder; **SF** recipes assume you're using soy-free chocolate chips, and so on).

INTRODUCTION

Introduction

Healthy Dessert: Is There Such a Thing?

These days, as more and more people seek a healthier lifestyle, finding a dessert that tastes great without contributing in some way to ill health can seem an impossible task. After all, isn't the term "healthy dessert" an oxymoron? We're hesitant to indulge, especially when so many conventional ingredients can be hazardous to our health: butter is high in saturated fat; eggs are loaded with cholesterol; milk is infused with allergy-inducing lactose or casein; refined sugars and flours have been stripped of almost all their nutrients. Yet we have to wonder, is it possible to enjoy authentic desserts without consuming any of these?

In the end, many of us throw up our hands in despair and vow to forgo our sweet treats. Or else we simply continue to eat the same baked goods and desserts we've enjoyed for years, swallowing our guilt along with the Death By Chocolate Brownie, in denial about the long-term, deleterious effects on our bodies. Delicious, appealing, and healthy treats seem to be the last unconquered frontier when it comes to today's health revolution.

With *Sweet Freedom*, I hope to prove that you can have your cake, and great health too! The desserts and other baked goods in this book were inspired by my own decision, after decades of baking and indulging in unhealthy sweets, to finally heed my body's wakeup call and radically alter my diet. Through years of both testing and selling the recipes to health food stores and farmers' markets, I've taken great care to ensure that every recipe you make from this book will taste just as good as a conventional dessert—and some, even better!

So read on, bake some amazing sweet treats, and indulge freely!

My Story

My mother was a traditional, naturally talented "from scratch" baker, and in one way or another, baking has been part of my life as long as I can remember. My dad, a dessert lover, was raised on a farm and couldn't tolerate "store-bought" foods. As a result, our home was perpetually filled with the aroma of some newly baked treat: soft and chewy chocolate chip cookies; warm, aromatic apple crumble cake; light and airy summertime cheesecake topped with fresh berries. And, of course, everyone knew about my mother's incredible, legendary Chiffon Cake, over ten inches high and made with *seven* eggs!

Consequently, I quickly became fascinated by what went on in the kitchen and baked my first batch of chocolate chip cookies, with my mom's help, at age six. I continued to bake—and eat—sweets regularly thereafter. In fact, my love of sugary sweets was the catalyst, ultimately, to bringing about a massive change in my diet and my devotion to a healthier lifestyle.

In my late twenties, after moving to a new city to attend graduate school, decades of poor eating habits finally caught up with me. I suddenly found myself unable to consume most of the foods I'd been accustomed to all my life. Even a single bite of bread would produce bloating, abdominal pain, or terrible constipation. After many unsuccessful visits to a wide variety of specialists, I was finally diagnosed with IBS (irritable bowel syndrome) and prescribed medication along with a high-fiber supplement. Typically, the doctor never suggested any changes in my eating habits.

Although the medication helped somewhat, my symptoms continued intermittently, and I went on eating the way I always had. I just assumed this was how I'd live the rest of my life, never knowing when or why my symptoms would flare up, and tried, dejectedly, to accept my lot. During this time, I continued to consume my favorite foods—chocolate, cookies, and cakes—and even began a small catering company that provided desserts for birthday parties, weddings, or company meetings.

Several years later, after a particularly bad bout of ill health that kept me off work for almost a month, I finally found my way to a naturopath. By then, I was so desperate I would have tried almost anything, so quickly agreed to the radical regimen she prescribed. The diet? No wheat, no eggs, no dairy, no sweeteners of any kind—and that was just to start! What was there left to eat? I was devastated, to say the least, but still determined to make a go of it and rid myself of my debilitating IBS symptoms.

I remember clearly arriving home from my first shopping trip to the health food store, bags of unfamiliar ingredients in hand, wondering if I'd ever get used to eating foreign foods like millet, tofu, or kale. Today, after following a whole-foods diet for over a decade, I'm happy to report that now many of the conventional food products are the ones that seem strange and unpalatable!

How *Sweet Freedom* Was Born

Even though I successfully avoided all sweeteners during the regimen and my health had improved remarkably, my love of desserts never wavered. While on the sweetener-free diet, I found creative ways to use fruits such as bananas or dates to produce at least a few dessert-like foods within the severe restrictions I was given. Unfortunately, after two years, when the "ban" on sweeteners was finally lifted, it didn't take long to revert to my old dietary habits. Suffering once again, I knew that I'd have to change my diet permanently to remain healthy.

Motivated by the powerful changes my naturopath had elicited, I took a leave of absence from my job to study natural nutrition and earn my RHN (Registered Holistic Nutritionist) designation. Before long, I was having a blast revamping old recipes and creating new ones to satisfy my sweet tooth. Knowing that any refined flours or sugars would throw me into binge mode, my new recipes used only unrefined and natural sweeteners, whole grain flours, and natural, whole ingredients. This means you won't find margarine (no matter if it's "non-hydrogenated"), refined white flours, refined sugars, or anything artificial, chemical-laden, or highly processed in my recipes.

And since they're all free of lactose, cholesterol, or any animal products, these recipes are all suitable for people with food sensitivities, lactose intolerance or anyone interested in animal-free foods (such as vegans or those on kosher diets).

Soon, I wanted to test out my new recipes on others, and decided to teach cooking classes in my home. I loved it! At the same time, following the principles I learned at nutrition school about whole, natural foods, I shed 25 pounds virtually without effort and finally weaned myself off the IBS medication I'd been taking for almost two decades. I'd never felt better!

The final chapter in my baking odyssey occurred that same year, one evening as I enjoyed dinner at a favorite vegetarian restaurant with my ultra-extroverted friend Judith. While chatting up the owner of the place, Judith discovered that he'd just lost his regular baker. Without hesitation, she enthused, "Well, Ricki's a great baker, and she's vegetarian, too!" The next thing I knew, I'd been hired to supply their desserts! In what seemed like no time, my creations sold out and became the subject of many requests, with people milling about as they waited for my weekly deliveries. Bolstered by this success and that of my cooking classes, I used many of my favorite recipes in 2005 to launch Bake It Healthy, an organic, all-natural custom bakery that specialized in baked goods free of wheat, eggs, dairy, or refined sweeteners.

Having sold these popular treats at health food stores and organic markets for a few years, I am delighted now to bring these recipes to you so that you can prepare and enjoy them in your own home.

How This Book Can Work For You

Even if you don't suffer from a major chronic condition like food sensitivities or IBS, baking with alternative ingredients is a great way to transform your diet into something that's simply better for your body—and ultimately, your well-being in general—without sacrificing familiar taste or satisfaction. Even better, you won't be consuming processed, chemical-laden foods that may promote ill health in the long run.

The recipes in *Sweet Freedom* are made with products available in most health-food stores or the natural foods section of your local supermarket. And while some of the ingredients, such as millet or agave nectar (a liquid sweetener derived from the agave cactus) may be unfamiliar, you won't see any hard-to-find items or totally "out there" recipes in this book—no seaweed cookies, miso frosting or maitake mushroom pudding. What you *will* find are many recipes for healthier versions of traditional favorites (such as frosted Vanilla Cupcakes, Banana-Nut Muffins, Chocolate Chip Cookies or Cinnamon Walnut Coffee Cake), as well as a huge array of desserts made with creative combinations of ingredients (yep, some vegetables, too) and innovative, unusual uses of alternatives to provide the greatest health benefits possible.

Where else would you find a recipe for moist, tantalizing Sweet Harvest Muffins (already a proven hit with both kids and adults), chock full of *three* kinds of vegetable, plus raisins and dark chocolate chips—and offering a full serving of vegetables in each muffin? Similarly, I know you'll enjoy the indulgent, yet heart-healthy Dark and Decadent Chocolate Pâté that combines the rich-tasting monounsaturated fats in avocado with the flavonoids in dark chocolate for an irresistible dessert. Because I love to experiment with novel uses of ingredients, I've also included recipes for Maple-Millet Muffins (with whole grains of crunchy, crispy rice-like millet), Pumpkinseed Shortbread Cookies (with zinc-rich pumpkinseed butter), Tomato Spice Cake (a traditional-tasting spice cake with puréed tomato) and Tropical Lemon and Coconut Muffins (with avocado as an egg substitute), plus many, many others.

The process of baking without wheat, eggs, dairy or refined sugar is a little different from that of conventional baking, so I've also included a chapter (following) on how to substitute whole grain flours, natural sweeteners, natural non-hydrogenated fats, and egg replacers in your existing recipes, as well as what to expect when cooking with these ingredients.

With just a few easy adjustments to your familiar routines, you *can* create foolproof desserts every bit as delicious as the ones you're used to—but without the saturated fats, cholesterol, lactose, or other health-depleting ingredients. As you'll quickly learn, a healthy lifestyle really *can* be sweet!

INGREDIENTS

and other

BAKING NOTES

Ingredients and Other Baking Notes

Baking with alternative ingredients need not be traumatic. So many whole-food ingredients out there work just as well as (if not better than) what's customary that there's no reason to use refined flours or sugars any more. Here's a list of the ingredients I generally use, and some tips to help make the transition as smooth as possible.

What if Not Wheat?

While it's true that our dependence on wheat has recently begun to wane with the media's push toward whole grains, for the most part we in the Western world are still so accustomed to using wheat in almost every baked good that at first we can't imagine anything otherwise. Yet wheat is only one of a plethora of grains available to us—some with gluten, some without—that are infinitely more nutritious, more easily digestible, and, in many cases, more tasty than wheat.

Wheat's Long-Lost Cousins, Spelt and Kamut

Spelt and kamut, both distant relatives of wheat, are ancient grains that have enjoyed a resurgence in popularity in the past few years. While both do contain gluten, they have less than wheat, and they haven't been hybridized the way wheat has over the years. As a result, spelt and kamut are often tolerated by people who are sensitive to wheat (such as myself).

Spelt is now available in both wholegrain ("whole" spelt) and partially refined ("light" spelt) varieties. While light spelt does retain less of the whole grain, it looks and acts much like all-purpose flour and is great in recipes requiring a lighter texture or more delicate crumb, such as vanilla cupcakes or lemon cake. Wholegrain spelt is made from the entire grain ground up, and looks and acts much like whole wheat flour.

Kamut flour is usually available only as whole grain. It's a bit more golden than spelt, with a nutty flavor. Because kamut is a "hard" flour (whereas spelt is "soft"), the kamut produces a more grainy, crumbly product. When I first started baking with alternatives, in order to approximate all-purpose wheat flour, I combined equal amounts of both spelt and kamut; nowadays, I favor mostly spelt because of its lighter texture, but must adjust for quantities when adapting existing recipes.

Spelt flour is available in health food stores, the natural foods section of most supermarkets, and in many bulk food stores.

> *To convert conventional recipes to spelt (this is a rough guide; you'll need to experiment to find exact substitutions):*
>
> You can substitute spelt for regular wheat flour with ease. For each cup (140 g) of all-purpose wheat flour, use 1 cup plus 2 Tbsp (160 g) light spelt flour, or 1 cup plus 3 Tbsp (160 g) whole spelt flour.

Whole Barley Flour

I love barley flour. I first discovered this flour as a result of reading the book *Simple Treats* by Ellen Abraham. Abraham baked wheat-free desserts using barley and whole oats (for the most part), and her goodies were comparable to conventional sweets. I find that barley flour (which is low-gluten), while a bit heavier than regular all-purpose flour, does produce a wonderful result, and its taste is neutral, like all-purpose. I often combine barley with spelt for a successful outcome, and because I want to add the wonderful nutritional qualities of the flour to my baking (barley is a great source of soluble fiber, which is known to help reduce "bad" cholesterol, it contributes to heart health, and it can help reduce the incidence of Type II Diabetes).

If you can't find barley flour where you live, you can substitute an equal amount of light spelt for the barley. The texture will be a little less delicate, but still quite tasty.

Barley flour is available in health food stores, the natural foods section of most supermarkets, and in bulk food stores.

> *To convert conventional recipes to barley (this is a rough guide; you'll need to experiment to find exact substitutions)*:
>
> You can substitute up to 1/3 of the original amount of all-purpose wheat flour in a recipe with an equal amount of barley without any radical change to the result. Or replace the original wheat flour with 2/3 spelt and 1/3 barley flours.

Whole Oat Flour

Much like barley flour, oat flour is made of the whole grains of oats, ground to a powder. Only recently have oats been deemed gluten free, even though they don't actually contain gluten; most conventional oats, however, have been cross-contaminated with wheat, and can't be consumed by those on a gluten-free diet. In recent years, however, certain brands of oats have been certified as gluten-free, grown in isolation from wheat (I find Bob's Red Mill brand to be reliable this way).

Because of its gluten-free nature, anything made with oat flour alone will crumble easily; as a result, I like to combine oat flour with other flours in baking to achieve a more tender crumb, but I use only part oat flour unless the item is meant to be entirely gluten-free.

If you can't find oat flour where you live, you can usually substitute a home-made version: simply grind up old-fashioned rolled oats in a blender or coffee grinder, to the texture of a powder or very fine meal. Use the same quantity as the oat flour called for in the recipe.

Oat flour is available in health food stores, some bulk stores, and in the natural foods section of some supermarkets.

> *To convert conventional recipes to oats (this is a rough guide; you'll need to experiment to find exact substitutions)*:
>
> I wouldn't recommend using oat flour in place of all-purpose wheat in recipes for the reason mentioned above: the result will be far too crumbly. You can, however, use oats in combination with wheat or spelt if you like. When replacing the original all-purpose wheat flour in a recipe, you can use up to 1/4 oat flour (and combine with 3/4 spelt flour if desired) for a successful result.

Other Flours

Although only about one third of my baking is entirely gluten-free, I do use GF flours on occasion to add texture or variety. Most of these flours are also available in health food stores, the natural foods section of most supermarkets, and in bulk food stores.

Because they don't contain gluten, GF flours require some other method to bind them together and replace the gluten that's missing. Most GF baking includes some kind of alternative binder, such as xanthan gum or guar gum, available as a powder and added in very small quantities (perhaps even 1/2 tsp or less per batch of baking). As a rule, I tend to avoid these kinds of binders, so most of my GF recipes are grain free.

Brown or White Rice Flours

Probably the most common gluten-free flour, rice flour produces a slightly grainy product that's great for scones or shortbread (in fact, traditional Scottish shortbread is made with rice flour). Baking with rice flour requires a bit of adjustment, and you should never simply substitute rice flour for all-purpose in any recipe.

Coconut Flour

Coconut flour is a relative newcomer on the market, made from the pulp left over after coconut oil is extracted from coconuts. It can be used to replace up to 1/3 of the regular flour in a recipe without noticeable changes to texture. It's also a high fiber flour (at 58% fiber, supposedly the highest percentage of any flour), and it absorbs liquid to some extent, so you can use it when you substitute liquid sweeteners for sugar in your recipes to compensate for the extra moisture.

These alternative flours are available in health food stores, some bulk stores, and in the natural foods section of some supermarkets.

A Sweet Alternative: Natural Sweeteners

Even though it provides virtually no nutritional value and the human body does not require it for health, most of us still love sugar. The average American consumes 159 pounds (72 kilos) of sugar and sweeteners per year (yes, the weight of an adult), and Canadians are likely not far behind.

Excessive sugar (and, in recent years, high fructose corn syrup) consumption results in lowered immunity and can lead to increased rates of obesity, Type II diabetes, heart disease, atherosclerosis (hardening of the arteries), osteoporosis, candida, chronic inflammation (which then leads to many other problems) and a host of other degenerative conditions. Given these results, no wonder sugar substitutes are so popular! Artificial sweeteners can be just as unhealthy. However, there are many natural alternatives you can use.

You'll find that natural sweeteners provide more nutrition than sugar and, often, better flavor, but do require some adjustments. Because natural sweeteners are usually liquid (with the exception of Sucanat, made from the sugar cane plant), you may need to adjust both the levels of other liquids in a recipe and the dry ingredients. All the recipes in this book have been designed with these properties in mind (and so, obviously, won't require any adjustments if followed as written). However, if you'd like to convert some of your older, sugar-filled recipes to those with natural sweeteners, then see below.

Agave Nectar

Derived from the juice of the agave cactus, agave nectar has been used for centuries in South America and Mexico and is the basis for tequila. It's 50% sweeter than sugar, yet has a very low GI (glycemic index), so it doesn't cause the same spikes in blood glucose levels that sugar does. In addition, the mild taste blends well with other flavors and won't overpower your recipes. Raw agave syrup also contains inulin, a "pre-biotic," or substance that helps to nourish the probiotics (good bacteria) in the intestines.

While it's been available much less time than any of the other sweeteners, agave has quickly become my favorite sweetener, not only because of its low GI, but also because of its mild flavor and versatility. Unlike honey, agave won't crystallize or stick to the bottom of the jar in which it's stored. If you're not fond of agave, you can usually substitute maple syrup in equal quantities (though maple syrup's flavor is much more prominent).

Most of my recipes will work with either dark or light agave nectar, and I'll mention this in the ingredients list. On some occasions, however (where the flavor must be very light or delicate), only light agave will do. In that case, you'll see only "light agave" mentioned in the ingredient list.

Agave nectar is available in health food stores, some bulk stores, and in the natural foods section of some supermarkets.

To convert conventional recipes to agave (this is a rough guide; you'll need to experiment to find exact substitutions):

When substituting agave for sugar, start with 2/3 cup (160 ml) agave for each cup (195 g) of sugar in the original recipe; if the result is too sweet for your taste, decrease to 1/2 cup (120 ml) next time. Because agave adds more liquid to the original recipe, also reduce any liquid ingredients by about 25%. For instance, if the original recipe calls for 1 cup (195 g) sugar and 1 cup (240 ml) milk, use 2/3 cup (160 ml) agave and only 3/4 cup (180 ml) milk (the rest of the recipe can stay the same).

If the original recipe doesn't contain any liquid at all, then add 25% more dry ingredients to the original recipe. For instance, if the original recipe calls for 1 cup (195 g) sugar and 1 cup (140 g) flour but no milk or other liquid, then use 2/3 cup (160 ml) agave and 1-1/4 (175 g) cups flour (the rest of the recipe can stay the same).

Blackstrap Molasses

Molasses is the residual product after sugar cane has been processed into cane (granulated) sugar. While the light, "Fancy" or "Barbados" varieties are formed early in the process and still retain a fairly high sugar content, blackstrap molasses contains very little sugar and actually retains all the nutrients that have been removed when sugar is made. The darker (or less sweet) the molasses, the more minerals it contains. Blackstrap molasses is the most nutritious form, with excellent levels of iron and calcium (two tablespoons contain more calcium than an 8-ounce glass of milk!) and good amounts of magnesium, potassium, and B-vitamins. Some people find the taste of blackstrap molasses too bitter (the unsulphured variety tastes best), so I always combine molasses with other sweeteners, and think of it as an addition rather than the main sweetener in any recipe.

Blackstrap molasses is available in health food stores, some bulk stores, and in the natural foods section of some supermarkets.

Maple syrup

The processed sap of the maple tree has a sweetness comparable to that of sugar, fewer calories and more minerals than honey, and the distinctive flavor beloved by many North Americans. It's an excellent source of manganese (a co-factor in many enzymatic actions in the body) as well as zinc (a key antioxidant vital to immune functioning and prostate health). The darker the syrup, the more its sugar has been concentrated. I love the flavor of maple syrup and find it complements certain other ingredients (such as walnuts or apples) beautifully.

Because of its high cost, however, it can be difficult to use maple syrup as the sole sweetener in any dish. If you can't get maple syrup or if you find the price prohibitive, it can usually be replaced with agave nectar in equal amounts in most recipes (though you'll lose that distinctive flavor, of course).

Maple syrup is available in most supermarkets and grocery stores, but you'll find a better quality product in health food stores or natural foods stores.

To convert conventional recipes to maple syrup (this is a rough guide; you'll need to experiment to find exact substitutions):

When substituting maple syrup for sugar, start with 2/3-3/4 cup (160-180 ml) syrup for each cup (195 g) of sugar in the original recipe. Because the syrup adds more liquid to the original recipe, also reduce any liquid ingredients by about 25-30%. For instance, if the original recipe calls for 1 cup (195 g) sugar and 1 cup (240 ml) milk, use 2/3 cup (160 ml) maple syrup and only 2/3-3/4 (160-180 ml) cups milk (the rest of the recipe can stay the same).

If the original recipe doesn't contain any liquid at all, then add 25-30% more dry ingredients to the original recipe. For instance, if the original recipe calls for 1 cup (195 g) sugar and 1 cup (140 g) flour but no milk or other liquid, then use 2/3 cup (160 ml) maple syrup and 1-1/4 to 1-1/3 cups (175-185 g) flour (the rest of the recipe can stay the same).

Brown Rice Syrup

This mildly-flavored, somewhat sweet syrup is made by culturing and cooking brown rice, then straining off the resulting sweet liquid. Compared to sugar, it is minimally processed and retains a high percentage of complex carbohydrates (unlike simple white sugar), which means it is digested and absorbed more slowly by the body, preventing spikes in blood glucose levels and allowing a steady, longer-term energy source. It also provides potassium and some B-vitamins.

To my palate, the flavor of brown rice syrup is reminiscent of caramel or butterscotch, so it's a perfect sweetener to use when you want to replicate that rich flavor. In addition, brown rice syrup is very thick and sticky, so it's ideal when you require more body in a dessert or are substituting for honey. It's not as sweet as the other natural sweeteners mentioned above, however, so you may not want to use it as your sole source of sweetness in a baked good (I usually combine it with one of the other sweeteners).

When replacing sugar with brown rice syrup, you'd need to add quite a bit more syrup because of its lower level of sweetness. For this reason, I rarely, if ever, make brown rice syrup the only sweetener in a recipe. You can, however, combine it with agave nectar or maple syrup.

Brown rice syrup is available in health food stores, some bulk stores, and in the natural foods section of some supermarkets.

Dates and other Fruit Purées

Because dates contain the highest natural sugar content of any fruit, I tend to use them as an additional source of sweetness in my baking. In addition, dates add moistness and a depth of flavor to chocolate-based desserts (such as the brownies in Dalmation Cheesecake Brownies or in Chocolate Mint Chocolate Chip Cookies).

You can use either plain (unsweetened) dried dates (sometimes called "cooking dates") or ready-made date purée in most of my recipes that call for dates. To make your own date purée, simply cover dates with boiling water and allow to soak for 20-30 minutes. Drain (reserve the liquid to use in other baked goods if you like) and process in a food processor until smooth. Store in covered containers in the refrigerator for up to 3 weeks, or freeze. (If using ready-made purée, be sure the only ingredients are dates and water).

This versatile fruit also adds essential nutrients such as iron, thiamine, riboflavin and niacin along with the bonus of high fiber (10 per cent of the daily requirement from just 5 dates). Other fruits that add sweetness on occasion include pears, apples, prunes or bananas.

Fruit purées make an excellent substitute for part of the sugar in a recipe, and can sometimes double for eggs or oil as well.

> *To convert conventional recipes to date purée (this is a rough guide; you'll need to experiment to find exact substitutions):*
>
> For each cup (195 g) of sugar in the original recipe, use up to 1/2 cup (120 ml) date purée plus 1/2 cup (90 g) Sucanat (see below). Reduce the original liquid by 2 Tbsp (30 ml).

Unrefined Evaporated Cane Juice or Dehydrated Cane Sugar Crystals

Sucanat or Rapadura, both forms of unrefined cane sugar, are made by evaporating or dehydrating the juice of the sugar cane plant without refining it first. The result is a dry, granular sweetener that can be used in the same proportions as sugar but which retains all of the original vitamins and minerals usually lost in processing (such as iron, calcium, vitamin B6, potassium and chromium, which can help to balance blood sugar). Watch for the word "unrefined" on the label, however; if the sweetener simply states, "evaporated cane juice," it may still be highly processed or refined.

I tend to use Sucanat because it's the brand I can get most easily and I love the flavor; but Rapadura may be substituted in equal quantities. I use this when a dry, crystalline sweetener is really essential.

One final note about using Sucanat: because its granules are larger than those of sugar, it doesn't dissolve quite as easily or quickly as white sugar. For that reason, I always add the Sucanat with my wet ingredients rather than the dry; that way, it begins to dissolve in the liquid before you mix it into the rest of the batter (you'll see that my recipes always call for adding Sucanat with the wet mixture).

Sucanat is available in health food stores, some bulk stores, and in the natural foods section of some supermarkets.

> *To convert conventional recipes to Sucanat (this is a rough guide; you'll need to experiment to find exact substitutions):*
>
> Sucanat can replace sugar in equal quantities when converting recipes. For each cup (195 g) of sugar in the original recipe, use one cup (180 g) of Sucanat. You can also substitute packed brown sugar for Sucanat in baking, though the nutritional properties will be different.

Stevia

The leaves of the *stevia rebaudiana* plant have been used as a sweetener for centuries in Latin America. Sold as Truvia® in the U.S. and as an herbal supplement in Canada, stevia is 30 times sweeter than sugar, yet boasts a GI of zero, so it doesn't affect blood sugar levels. Most alternative health professionals such as naturopaths or holistic nutritionists recommend stevia as a healthy alternative to sugar. You can buy stevia as a liquid or powder.

While it adds a great deal of sweetness to foods and I use it often (for example, to sweeten my oatmeal or smoothies in the morning, in some salad dressings or in teas), it cannot be substituted for sugar in baking without greatly altering a recipe's texture. Use where only small amounts of sugar would do. I tend not to use stevia simply because of the change in volume and texture it would cause to the ingredients.

Stevia is available in health food stores, some bulk stores, and in the natural foods section of some supermarkets.

Natural Egg Substitutes

There exist a large variety of ways to compensate for eggs in baking; any vegan baker is already familiar with these, including pre-packaged substitutes such as Ener-G egg replacer powder.

Because I use (as much as possible) only natural, whole foods and ingredients, I'm not overly fond of the pre-packaged or powdered replacers such as Ener-G (which contains carbohydrate gum and chemical leaveners).

Instead, I usually opt for one of the following to replace eggs:

Flax Seeds

Flax seeds are a high source of healthy Omega 3 fats and add protein, fat, and fiber to your baking. When ground flax seeds are mixed with water, they develop a viscous, gel-like texture that resembles that of raw egg whites. They can also be used successfully to replace the binding power of eggs in baking (though you'll need to add more leaveners when using flax eggs).

I tend to use ground flax more than any other egg substitute, as flax seeds are fairly easy to find (most bulk or health foods stores now carry them) and reasonably priced. You can certainly buy pre-ground flax meal, but I find the cost isn't worth it; I purchase whole seeds (which can be stored at room temperature), grind them in a coffee grinder, and use as needed. (Because of the high omega-3 content in flax, however, you should always store any ground seeds in a dark container in the refrigerator or freezer; keep no more than 6 weeks this way. If buying pre-ground seeds, opt for the vacuum-packed bags, and then store opened bags in the freezer or refrigerator).

Note: Since my recipes have already been formulated to account for the moisture absorbed by the flax, there is no need to make any changes when you see flax in these recipes.

Flax seeds are available in health food stores, some bulk stores, and in the natural foods section of some supermarkets.

Ground Chia Seeds

Chia is a more recent addition to the high-Omega 3 group of foods. With an Omega-3 content, protein content, and fiber content even higher than those of flax, chia has been touted as the next super-food. One of the great qualities of chia for my purposes, however, is that, once ground, it makes a wonderful egg substitute that can also absorb a fair amount of liquid in a recipe.

Although chia is more expensive than flax, I've become quite enamored of the tiny white or grey seeds. Once ground, they form a fine powder, which is less visible than flax in the final product. They also retain moisture differently from flax seeds, resulting in a more tender crumb for baked goods.

I use chia in some recipes for more delicate results (such as the Holiday Apple Cake or Tomato Spice Cake), but *you can always use flax as a substitute for chia in any recipe*; use one tablespoon (15 ml) ground flax to replace each teaspoon (5 ml) of ground chia in my recipes. The resultant product will have a slightly denser texture, however.

Chia seeds are available in health food stores, some bulk stores, and in the natural foods section of some supermarkets

Silken Tofu

Silken tofu usually comes water-packed in a plastic tub in the refrigerated section of your supermarket. This Chinese-style (with water) is a great egg substitute, as is the soft silken

Japanese style (packed in non-refrigerated, aseptically sealed tetra-pack boxes). Either form works well.

A key quality of silken tofu is its resemblance in both appearance and texture to custard. As a result, when used in baking, this firm, custard-like texture helps to bind and firm up the baked good in question. It's also moister than flax or chia, so is often used in cookies or squares that require moistness, such as brownies. And silken tofu is a great "cheesecake" base.

I'd recommend using only organic brands of tofu if at all possible, however, since some brands may contain genetically modified (GMO) soybeans otherwise, which are not always identified on the label (organic products by law can't contain GMOs, so they are a safer bet).

While tofu has been proven a great source of protein and helpful to alleviate some cardiovascular problems as well as symptoms associated with menopause, some health food advocates recommend avoiding tofu because it can cause digestive problems or issues for those with low thyroid function. Because I don't have these reactions to tofu, I feel comfortable using it in moderation. Of course, you should do what feels right to you. Any of the other egg substitutes listed here can be used to replace tofu "eggs" in my recipes.

Tofu is available in health food stores, some bulk stores, and in the natural foods section of some supermarkets (though many conventional brands in supermarkets aren't organic).

To convert conventional recipes to tofu eggs:

For each egg you wish to replace, use 1/4 cup (60 ml) packed silken tofu; simply scoop the tofu from the package and into a 1/4 cup (60 ml) measuring cup, pressing down and chopping it up with a spoon to eliminate any air pockets. Because it will hold its shape, silken tofu must be puréed in a food processor or blender before being added to any batter; my recipes usually include this step in the preparation of the wet ingredients.

Fruit Purées

Many bakers use fruit purées instead of eggs in their baking, as these add moistness and help the batter to bind together. As a general rule, about 1/4 cup (60 ml) of any purée equals one egg. I tend not to use fruit purées as the only egg substitute in my baking, as I find they alter the flavor of the product significantly (in general, you'll be able to taste if banana has been added to your baked good, for instance). However, I do use purées where the flavor and texture will complement the original recipe, such as in banana bread, brownies, and so on.

Avocado

Yes, avocado is technically a fruit, but since most people don't think of it that way, I've decided to mention it in a distinct category!

I've recently discovered that avocado purée can act as a wonderful egg substitute in certain dishes; avocado confers moistness, body, and healthy fat. Because avocados are already high in monounsaturated (heart-healthy) fats, they can be used to replace some of the other oils in your baking as well. I tend to use avocado where its flavor and color won't be detected (such as in the Ultra Fudgy Brownies), but it's also been useful in some other boldly-flavored recipes (such as the Tropical Lemon Coconut Muffins). About 1/4 cup (60 ml) packed avocado purée replaces one egg.

Better Fats and Oils

After learning about the various chemical structures of most cooking oils and how they react to heat while I was in nutrition school, I began to narrow down my choices for fats that I'd comfortably use in baking. My list of preferred fats and oils for baked goods is probably shorter than the one you're used to, and certainly, you're welcome to use almost any oil in these recipes and the flavor and texture won't change dramatically. If your purpose is to prevent damage to the chemical structure and nutritional qualities of the oil, however, you might like to read on.

Coconut Oil

For years, coconut oil received a "bad rap" because of its high saturated fat content; it was also, in the past, often hydrogenated. Today, however, high-quality, unrefined (also called "extra virgin") and organic coconut oils are an ideal butter substitute for those who don't eat dairy. Like butter, coconut oil is solid at room temperature (it melts at 76F or 24.5C), and, depending on the brand you buy, need not add a "coconut" flavor to your baked good.

The best characteristic of coconut oil, however, is that (as a naturally saturated fat) it is "safe" to use with relatively high heat. Undamaged by the heat of baking, coconut oil will preserve the integrity of the baked good where other fats might not. And, unlike animal-based saturated fats, coconut oil has been shown in some studies to help improve cholesterol levels and heart health rather than destroy them.

Use coconut oil in the same quantities as butter in a recipe. When substituting for butter, your coconut oil should be soft, but still solid. In recipes that require the oil to be melted first, I'll state that in the recipe.

Olive Oil

A source of healthy monounsaturated fat, olive oil would be my first choice of oil for baking, as it can withstand higher heats than most other oils. A good quality, unrefined and cold-pressed olive oil, however, will taste like its source—olives. So I confine my use of olive oil to those recipes where there is very little oil (about 2 Tbsp or 30 ml) per recipe, or where the other flavors in the recipe are strong enough that the olive flavor won't be detected. If you like the flavor, feel free to use an equal amount of olive oil wherever sunflower oil is mentioned in my recipes.

Sunflower Oil

Sunflower oil is the oil I use most often, and the main liquid oil mentioned in my recipes. It's a light-tasting oil that produces lovely results; however, as a polyunsaturated oil, it can be somewhat damaged by heat. Still, because some recipes absolutely require a liquid (rather than solid) fat, sunflower oil works best in those situations. It's also the most affordable of the types of oil I use. If you can find high-oleic sunflower oil, buy that, as it is hardier.

Why not canola?

Most people are surprised to discover that I don't use canola oil in my baking. Although it is a polyunsaturated oil, many brands of canola, if not organic, tend to contain GMO (genetically modified) ingredients, or have been highly processed to remove a strong flavor (and even some of the organic varieties may be cross-contaminated with GMO crops). Because of the tendency toward so much processing, I prefer not to use canola oil in my cooking and baking.

Alternatives to Cow's Milk

Nowadays, there are so many varieties of alternative milk in stores that even if you don't drink them, you're probably aware of soymilk and perhaps rice milk. While all can be useful as an alternative in daily cooking, I've found that the properties of different milks create different results in baked goods.

Here are some of the more common milk substitutes I use, and where they're most useful.

Soymilk

Soymilk is probably the most well-known milk alternative, as well as the most popular. Despite some recent controversies about the problems with soy for children, those with low thyroid, or people with cancer (see "tofu," above), I believe that, used in moderation, organic soymilk can be a great addition to baked goods and desserts. Because of its relatively high protein content, it seems to work in baking much like cow's milk does, and produces similar results.

In general, I use unsweetened, "plain," or "original" flavors for baking. You can use soymilk one for one instead of cow's milk.

Almond Milk

Made from boiled, crushed and strained almonds, almond milk is a wonderful alternative for those avoiding soy (though it is a bit more expensive than soymilk). It can be used anywhere soymilk is used. As with soymilk, I tend to use unsweetened or "original" flavors. Use one for one with cow's milk or soymilk.

Rice Milk

While it's probably my favorite in terms of taste, rice milk is quite a bit thinner than soy or almond milk, and so isn't a perfect replacement for either of those in baked goods; the resultant product is sometimes a bit too light or delicate, and may crumble easily. In other instances (such as the Coconut Whipped "Cream"), it is actually a better alternative, when a light and airy texture is preferred. One advantage of rice milk is that it rarely contains added sugar, since the rice itself produces a relatively sweet taste.

If you do use rice milk instead of soy or almond in these recipes, be aware that your final product may lack the intended density.

Coconut Milk

While I find coconut milk too rich to use as a one for one replacement with soy or almond milk, it's great in certain recipes where a rich, creamy outcome is required (such as the whipped cream, above, or puddings, "cheese" cakes, and so on). For a more tender, richer cake or cupcake, a mix of half coconut milk and half another alternative milk works beautifully. As with coconut oil, organic coconut milk is your best choice for the highest quality.

Other Key Ingredients

Nuts and Seeds

Fresh, organic nuts and seeds are wonderful sources of protein and healthy fats (both mono- and polyunsaturated). However, with this high fat content comes the same caveat as with cooking oils, above: because toxins reside in fats, buy organic whenever possible. In addition, pre-roasted nuts and seeds are often cooked in unhealthy fats (and lots of added salt), and their lack of freshness may be concealed under their toasty exterior.

If possible, I'd recommend buying raw, unsalted nuts and seeds and roasting them yourself. Also buy whole nuts whenever possible; the smaller the pieces (for instance, pre-chopped nuts), the more surface area has been exposed to air, heat, or light, all of which damage the fragile fats that have been exposed.

To roast them, I spread a single layer of nuts or seeds in a rimmed cookie sheet (or use a square or rectangular cake pan) and bake at 350F (180C) for 10-15 minutes, until just golden and fragrant. Cool and store, covered, in the refrigerator, up to a month.

Nut and Seed Butters

Home-roasted nuts and seeds make a perfect base for homemade nut or seed butters, which are much fresher and less expensive than the store-bought variety (of course, I do keep jars of ready-made almond and cashew butters on hand for when I haven't the time or inclination to make my own—they work just fine in all the recipes!).

Another reason I favor homemade nut butters over store-bought is that I can control the amount of salt and the texture; the homemade variety is a bit thicker and spreads more easily than the jarred type (I find that prepared nut butters are sometimes a bit runny). In addition, I can blend a few different types of nuts in one nut butter according to my taste, rather than rely on just "almond" or "cashew" butter. (One great combination I use is a ratio of 1/2 almonds and 1/4 each cashews and walnuts or pecans).

> *To make nut or seed butter:* simply place toasted, cooled nuts or seeds in a powerful food processor and process until crumbly. Then keep processing until the mixture becomes finer and eventually forms a ball that rolls around the processor bowl; keep processing past this point, and the ball will eventually smooth out and become nut butter. You'll need to stop periodically and scrape the sides of the processor, and will also require patience—it can take up to 10 minutes—but the result is worth it. Store in clean jars in the refrigerator.

Cocoa Powder

Unsweetened cocoa, a powder made from the cacao bean, is bitter on its own. Many bakers prefer to use Dutch process cocoa, as it offers a milder flavor and supposedly results in a finer textured baked good. I always opt for the darkest cocoa I can find, and one that is *not* Dutch process (or alkalized), as the darker powder, like dark chocolate, contains more flavonoids (compounds with antioxidant-like properties) than the lighter, alkalized type. This is one instance when the less expensive option is actually the better choice!

Chocolate Chips:

My recipes call for dark, dairy-free chocolate chips; however, conventional chocolate chips do contain sugar. If you wish to keep the recipes entirely sugar-free, opt for grain-sweetened chips (the brand I use is Sunspire). They are a little less sweet than conventional chips, but taste great nonetheless.

Instant Coffee Substitute

I like Krakus brand to produce a coffee-like taste in my baked goods, but any brand of coffee substitute will do. You might have to adjust the amount with other brands, as Krakus is very mild (which is why I like it). Of course, you can always use actual instant coffee where my recipes call for the caffeine-free substitutes. If converting to instant coffee instead of the coffee substitute in my recipes, use about half as much coffee (that is, one tsp (5 ml) coffee to replace 2 tsp (10 ml) coffee substitute).

Baking Measures, Methods and Equipment

Measuring for Best Results

My recipes are based on specific combinations of ingredients and will work best when the measurements are exactly the same as those in the recipes. It's worth noting how I measure my ingredients, as I've learned that not everyone automatically uses the same methods I do. To achieve the best results, I'd recommend following these guidelines.

For dry ingredients (such as flour) and thick moist ingredients (such as nut butters): I use individual metal or plastic measuring cups in incremental amounts of 1/8 cup (equivalent to 2 Tbsp or 30 ml), 1/4 cup (equivalent to 4 Tbsp or 60 ml), 1/2 cup (equivalent to 8 Tbsp or 120 ml) and 1 cup (equivalent to 16 Tbsp or 240 ml).

To measure, I scoop the cup into the dry ingredient, then level the top with the back of a knife. I don't pack down the dry contents by shaking the cup. (When using metric measures, I simply weigh the dry ingredients). I measure small amounts of dry ingredients (baking powder, salt, etc.) the same way, using a tablespoon or teaspoon and leveling the top.

I also always sift my dry ingredients after measuring them (to break up any small lumps) by pushing them through a fine mesh sieve. You can also stir the dry ingredients with a whisk for the same effect.

For moist ingredients: I scoop the nut butter (or coconut oil or silken tofu, etc.) into the cup and pack it in with the back of a spoon to eliminate air pockets; then I level the top, as above.

For liquid ingredients (such as milk or oil): I pour the ingredient into a clear, 2-cup (500 ml) capacity measuring cup, stopping when the liquid reaches the desired amount if viewed at eye level.

I also always scrape out the cups as cleanly as possible with a rubber or silicon spatula (even the last drops of milk or oil from a glass measuring cup!).

A Note About Metric Measurements

When converting from Imperial to Metric measures, I've used the following methods:

Dry ingredients: measured by weight (grams), except for smaller amounts (less than 60 ml), which are measured by volume (milliliters).

Wet ingredients (including silken tofu and nut butters): measured by volume (milliliters).

In browsing through the recipes, you may notice that the metric conversions don't always appear consistent from one recipe to another (for instance, 1/4 cup oats is converted as 30 g, but 1/2 cup is 50 g). The variation is a result of my measuring, and converting, each recipe one at a time, as I prepare them. Because measuring by volume is not an exact science, 1/4 cup of oats may result in 28 grams, while 1/2 cup might weigh in at 52 grams. In each case, I rounded up or down to the nearest 5 gram mark. Rest assured that I've tested each of the recipes several times using both Imperial and Metric measurements, so you can be confident that the amounts listed will result in the best outcome for each recipe, whichever method you use.

Special Equipment: I Love My Food Processor! (and a Nifty Trick)

I hadn't realized how much I use my food processor in these recipes until I started typing them out for the book. A good food processor is indispensable for some of the desserts (particularly the cheesecakes and those involving softened dates as a sweetener), and I often use it as a single vessel in which to mix the entire batter in a recipe. Mine is a Cuisinart 11-cup (about 2-1/2 liter) capacity machine. However, any good processor will work for these recipes, and most can still be made successfully without one, as long as you're willing to give the muscles in your forearms a good workout.

And in case you haven't heard this one before, here's a nifty trick for scraping out all the contents of the processor and cleaning off the blades in a snap: when working with thick or sticky batters (such as cakes or brownies), simply scrape out as much as you can into your mixing bowl or pan, but don't worry too much about the blades. Place the almost-clean bowl back on the base, leaving the blades inside. Cover once more and process for a few seconds; the centrifugal force of the spinning blades will throw any excess batter onto the walls of the processor bowl, leaving the blades virtually clean. Then open it up again, remove the blades, and scrape out the last bits of your batter from the processor bowl.

Testing the Doneness of Natural Baked Goods

The traditional toothpick-in-center test for baked goods won't work for most of the recipes in this book, as batters based on whole grains are already fairly dark or golden, and darken even more when baked; the color is so close to that of a toothpick that you might not be able to distinguish the batter from the wood. Instead, I use a small, very sharp steak knife and insert it in the center of the cake, muffin, or cupcake. If the knife comes out clean, it's ready. I find this method fairly easy—and it provides a good use for my otherwise unused steak knives! (Of course, a metal skewer will work well, too).

Storing Your Natural Baked Goods

Unlike conventional baked goods, *Sweet Freedom's* recipes don't contain preservatives or sugar (which acts as a natural preservative). In addition, moist sweeteners such as agave nectar or brown rice syrup can begin to ferment if kept too long at room temperature. Consequently, it's best to store your baked goods in the refrigerator (in a closed container or tightly wrapped with plastic) to prevent drying out. For items that are best eaten at room temperature, simply remove them from the fridge 20-30 minutes before serving. Most of the baked goods will keep for 4-5 days in the refrigerator, and can be frozen for longer periods (recipes will indicate which items can be frozen).

BREAKFAST BAKING:

MUFFINS,

SCONES, ROLLS

and the LIKE

Maple Millet Muffins

recipe, page 47

Carob and Date Pancakes

recipe, page 38

Zucchini and Pineapple

Mini Loaves or Muffins

recipe, page 66

Breakfast Baking: Muffins, Scones, Rolls and the Like

Maybe it's because I'm a morning person, but breakfast is definitely my favorite meal of the day. And why not? A good breakfast contains all the major nutrients—complex carbohydrates, proteins, and healthy fats. In fact, I've often thought that there's no better dinner than a good breakfast!

Over the years, I've developed recipes for breakfast breads, muffins, scones, and loaves that are easy to make, delicious, and substantial enough to carry you through the day.

For many people, pancakes represent the quintessential weekend fare. The varieties shared here won't disappoint. Fluffy Fruited Pancakes are a sterling example, with mixed berries and a boost of extra protein powder in a light and airy base. Or opt for some quick and easy Corn Crêpes or Carob and Date Pancakes for a substantial accompaniment to Sunday brunch.

Muffins are the perfect portable breakfast, but many of the ones you find in supermarkets or coffee shops are high in fat and refined ingredients. You'll discover that the healthy muffins included here are surprisingly light and moist, even without the extra oils. And they all work wonderfully with a light coat of nut butter or fruity jam.

Bake It Healthy's best-seller, the Sweet Harvest Muffin, will amaze you with its subtle melding of spice and sweetness, and full serving of vegetables in each delicious muffin. Or go for the Orange Oat Muffins with their chewy oats and whole orange puréed into the batter. Two banana-based muffins are also on the list: moist and raisin-studded Oatbran Banana Muffins, or the light and tender Banana Nut version. A favorite of mine are the Tropical Lemon Coconut Muffins, pairing hidden avocado with coconut and the tang of fresh lemon. Who could imagine a better breakfast on the go?

For those who prefer rolls or bread-based breakfasts, you'll find plenty of those, too. Sweet and gooey Cinnamon Buns are a true indulgence, one that you might like to share with friends or guests. In fact, nothing beats the French Toast Soufflé with Summer Berries when you're entertaining; it's the ideal contribution to a brunch buffet or pot luck. For everyday breakfasts, try some yummy Orange Raisin Tea Cakes or Oatmeal Walnut Scones. Or how about a thick slice of moist Irish Poppyseed Bread with a slathering of almond butter?

Whatever your breakfast pleasure, you'll find something to fulfill your taste buds here. And don't forget that these treats will also taste just as delicious later on, at noon or six p.m.!

Banana Chocolate Chip Mini-Loaves or Muffins

These are a nice change from regular banana bread, with a slightly lighter texture and the addition of chocolate chips for a more dessert-like feel.

1 cup (265 g) banana purée (2-3 medium bananas)
1/3 cup (80 ml) light agave nectar
Scant 1/4 cup (60 ml) sunflower or other light-tasting oil, preferably organic
2 Tbsp (30 ml) finely ground flax seeds
2 Tbsp (30 ml) water
1 tsp (5 ml) pure vanilla extract
1/3 cup (135 g) dairy-free chocolate chips
1 cup (140 g) light spelt flour
1/2 cup (70 g) whole spelt flour
1-1/2 tsp (7.5 ml) baking powder
1/2 tsp (2.5 ml) baking soda
1/8 tsp (.5 ml) fine sea salt

Preheat oven to 350F (180C). Line 8 mini loaf pans or 10 muffin cups with paper liners, or spray with nonstick spray.

In a medium-sized bowl, combine the banana purée, agave nectar, oil, flax seeds, water and vanilla. Stir in the chocolate chips, and set aside while you prepare the dry ingredients (or at least 2 minutes).

In a large bowl, sift together the light spelt flour, whole spelt flour, baking powder, baking soda, and salt. Add the wet mixture to the dry and stir to blend (it's okay if a few dry spots are left here and there). The batter will be fairly thin.

Using a large ice cream scoop or 1/3 cup (80 ml) measuring cup, turn the batter into the mini loaf pans, filling about 3/4 full. Bake in preheated oven for 25-30 minutes, rotating pan about halfway through, until tops are golden and a tester inserted in a center loaf comes out clean. Makes 8 loaves or 10 muffins. May be frozen.

> **Variation**: Substitute nuts or toasted sunflower seeds for the chocolate chips.

Banana Nut Muffins

These muffins are ideal for breakfast—moist, light, and with some built-in healthy protein and fats from the flaxseeds and walnuts or pecans. I love these with a little bit of almond butter.

- **3 very ripe medium bananas (about 1 cup or 265 g), mashed**
- **1/4 cup plus 2 Tbsp (90 ml) pure maple syrup**
- **2 Tbsp (30 ml) finely ground flax seeds**
- **1 tsp (5 ml) pure vanilla extract**
- **1/2 tsp (2.5 ml) apple cider vinegar**
- **1/3 cup (80 ml) sunflower or other light-tasting oil, preferably organic**
- **2 Tbsp (30 ml) plain or vanilla soy or almond milk (or a splash more if batter is dry)**
- **1/2 cup (50 g) chopped pecans**
- **1-3/4 cups (250 g) light spelt flour**
- **2 tsp (10 ml) baking powder**
- **1/2 tsp (2.5 ml) baking soda**
- **1/4 tsp (1 ml) fine sea salt**

Preheat oven to 375F (190C). Line 9 muffin cups with paper liners for large muffins or 12 cups for small muffins, or spray with nonstick spray.

In a medium bowl, combine the bananas, maple syrup, flax seeds, vanilla, vinegar, oil and milk; whisk to blend well, then stir in the pecans. Set aside while you measure dry ingredients, or at least 2 minutes.

In a large bowl, sift the flour, baking powder, baking soda and salt. Pour the wet ingredients over the dry and stir just to blend (it's okay if a few small dry spots remain here and there).

Using a large ice cream scoop or 1/3 cup (80 ml) measuring cup, fill the muffin cups about 3/4 full for small muffins or completely full for large muffins (these will not rise much during baking).

Bake in preheated oven for 25-30 minutes, rotating pan about halfway through, until muffins are beginning to brown on top and a tester inserted in a center muffin comes out clean. Allow to cool 5 minutes before removing to a rack to cool completely. Store tightly covered or wrapped in plastic in refrigerator for up to 5 days. May be frozen.

Carob and Date Pancakes

These were a spontaneous invention one Sunday morning when I craved pancakes and wanted to try something different. The bonus is they're high in calcium and other minerals—only 2 pancakes offer up 215 grams of calcium!

- **1-3/4 cups (420 ml) plain or vanilla soy or almond milk**
- **2 Tbsp (30 ml) finely ground flax seeds**
- **2 tsp (10 ml) apple cider vinegar**
- **1/4 cup (60 ml) sunflower or other light-tasting oil, preferably organic**
- **2 Tbsp (30 ml) pure maple syrup**
- **2/3 cup (80 g) coarsely chopped dried dates (they should be soft)**
- **2 cups (270 g) whole spelt flour**
- **3 Tbsp (45 ml) carob flour or powder**
- **1 Tbsp (15 ml) baking powder**
- **1/2 tsp (2.5 ml) baking soda**
- **1/4 tsp (1 ml) fine sea salt**
- **1/4 tsp (1 ml) ground cardamom (optional)**

In a small bowl, combine the soymilk, flax seeds, vinegar, oil, maple syrup and chopped dates. Set aside while you measure the dry ingredients, or at least 2 minutes.

In a large bowl, sift the spelt flour, carob powder, baking powder, soda, salt and cardamom, if using. (Note: even if you don't normally sift your flour, you should sift the carob powder, as it tends to clump up in the batter otherwise, leaving hard little lumps).

Pour the wet mixture over the dry and mix well. It may seem a bit thin; this is as it should be.

Heat a nonstick frypan over medium heat; spray with olive oil or nonstick spray. Using a medium ice cream scoop or 1/4 cup (60 ml) measuring cup, scoop the batter (taking care to include a few bits of date in each pancake) and pour onto hot pan. Spread a little with the back of the scoop to create an even thickness.

Cook the pancakes until bubbles break on the surface and the outside edge is dry and just beginning to brown (3-4 minutes). Flip and cook the other side 2-3 more minutes. Repeat until all the batter is used. Makes about 12 pancakes. Garnish with chopped pecans just before serving, if desired. May be frozen.

Cashew Date Bread

This couldn't properly be called "banana bread" because the banana flavor is so subtle that it might go unnoticed. It does add sweetness and moistness to the bread, however, which is rich with soft dates and crunchy cashews. If you find the sesame flavor of the tahini too pronounced, you can replace some or all of it with another seed butter (such as sunflower seed butter) or peanut butter.

- **7-1/2 ounces (215 g) very ripe banana (about 2 large bananas), mashed**
- **1/3 cup (80 ml) tahini (sesame seed paste)**
- **1/3 cup (80 ml) agave nectar, light or dark**
- **1 Tbsp (15 ml) finely ground flax seeds**
- **1/3 cup (80 ml) water**
- **2 Tbsp (30 ml) sunflower or other light-tasting oil, preferably organic**
- **1 tsp (5 ml) pure vanilla extract**
- **1 cup (120 g) coarsely chopped dates**
- **1/3 cup (55 g) coarsely chopped unsalted cashews**
- **3/4 cup (105 g) whole spelt flour**
- **1 cup (140 g) light spelt flour**
- **1 tsp (5 ml) baking soda**
- **1-1/4 tsp (6 ml) baking powder**
- **1/2 tsp (2.5 ml) fine sea salt**

Preheat oven to 350F (180C). Line an 8" (20 cm) loaf pan with parchment paper, or spray with nonstick spray.

In a medium bowl, mash the banana. Add the tahini, agave nectar, flax seeds, water, oil and vanilla and whisk well or beat with electric beaters until well blended and the tahini is perfectly incorporated without any lumps remaining. (Alternately, place all the ingredients in a food processor and whir together until smooth). Fold in the dates and cashews. Set aside while you measure the dry ingredients, or at least 2 minutes.

In a large bowl, sift together the whole spelt flour, light spelt flour, baking soda, baking powder and salt. Pour the wet mixture over the dry and stir just to combine (don't worry if there are a few small dry spots here and there). The batter will be fairly thick.

Turn the batter into the prepared loaf pan and smooth the top. Bake in preheated oven for 50 minutes to an hour, rotating pan about halfway through, until a tester inserted in the center comes out moist but clean. (If the top of the loaf begins to brown too much before it tests ready, cover with aluminum foil for the last 10 minutes of baking).

Cool in pan for 10 minutes before turning out onto a rack to cool completely. Makes 8-10 servings. May be frozen.

> **Variation:** Use other nuts, such as chopped almonds or pecans, instead of the cashews. If you're not a fan of tahini, you can substitute almond butter here as well (though the flavor will change slightly, of course).

Cinnamon Buns

This yeast-free recipe yields buns that are light, tender, and oozing with gooey cinnamon filling. They are a little bit of work, but well worth it: topped with the optional glaze, these are as decadent as any ultra-rich dessert.

Filling:
1/2 cup (90 g) Sucanat (or other unrefined evaporated cane juice)

2 Tbsp (15 g) whole spelt flour

2 Tbsp (30 ml) ground cinnamon (yes, tablespoons—don't worry, it's not overpowering)

3 Tbsp (45 ml) sunflower or other light-tasting oil, preferably organic

1 Tbsp (15 ml) water, plus up to 2 more teaspoons (10 ml) if necessary

Dough:
2 cups plus 2 Tbsp (300 g) light spelt flour

1 cup (135 g) whole spelt flour, plus 2 Tbsp (30 ml) more if necessary (plus 1/4-1/2 cup more for dusting and rolling out dough)

2 Tbsp (30 ml) baking powder

1/2 tsp (2.5 ml) fine sea salt

1/4 cup (60 ml) chilled coconut oil, preferably organic (should be solid)

1 cup (240 ml) pure orange juice (see tip 1)

2 Tbsp (30 ml) light agave nectar

Glaze (optional):
1/2 cup (90 g) Sucanat (or other unrefined evaporated cane juice)

1/4 cup (30 g) organic cornstarch

Up to 2 Tbsp (30 ml) plain or vanilla rice , soy or almond milk

Preheat oven to 350F (180C). Line a 9" (22.5 cm) springform pan with parchment paper, or spray with nonstick spray (alternately, you may use one 8" (20 cm) square pan and one standard loaf pan; line or spray both pans as well). Have ready a rectangular cutting board, plastic placemat, or piece of waxed paper that's about 13 inches by 10 inches (32 x 26 cm) big.

Make the filling first: In a medium bowl, combine the Sucanat, 2 Tbsp (30 ml) whole spelt flour and cinnamon; mix well. Drizzle the oil over top and stir to combine and coat as much of the filling as possible. Add one tablespoon (15 ml) water and mix it in completely to create a thick but spreadable paste (it should not become liquid at all, but be more the texture of a nut butter). If mixture is too thick, add more liquid one teaspoon at a time; be careful not too add to much liquid, or the filling will be too thin! Set aside.

Make the dough: In a large bowl, sift together the light spelt flour, 1 cup (135 g) whole spelt flour, baking powder and salt; use a whisk or fork to mix together. Drop the cold coconut oil by teaspoons (5 ml) over the surface of the dry mixture. Using a pastry cutter or wide-tined fork, cut the mixture by pressing through the lumps of coconut oil and into the flour, just enough to create pea-sized pieces of oil (some bits may be smaller, but none should be larger). Toss the flour mixture with a fork to distribute the oil throughout. Resist the temptation to pinch this together with your fingers as you would a crumb topping; the oil should **not** be completely blended in to the flour mixture, but just scattered throughout in little lumps. Set aside.

In a glass measuring cup, whisk the juice with the agave nectar. Pour this wet mixture over the dry ingredients in the bowl and toss with a fork until it comes together in a ball (again, avoid touching this with your hands, except to pull it away from the sides of the bowl and push it together in a ball). You should have a very soft and moist dough; this is as it should be. If it is too moist to hold together, add the extra 2 Tbsp (30 ml) whole spelt flour and combine quickly.

Flour the cutting board, placemat, or waxed paper with about 1/4 cup (35 g) more whole spelt flour. Place the mound of dough on the board, pushing it into a ball with your hands, and dust the top of the ball with about 2 Tbsp (30 ml) more whole spelt flour. With a floured rolling pin, roll out the dough so it more or less covers the rectangle, starting in the middle and rolling toward the edges (see tip 2).

Spread the filling over the rectangle with a rubber spatula, coming right to the edge on three sides, and leaving a one-inch (2.5 cm) border of dough on one of the longer sides. Begin to roll the dough, starting at the long side that has filling right up to the edge, and roll toward the long side with the one-inch empty border. Once you get to the end, keep rolling so that the last long edge (the "seam") is underneath the roll. Cut the roll into 3 equal pieces (you can measure them, or just estimate—it doesn't need to be perfect). Then cut each piece into 3 more equal pieces, for 9 pieces total. Each piece will become one bun.

Place the pieces in the round pan so that the spiral pattern is facing up (that is, one of the cut edges is against the bottom of the pan and the other cut edge faces upward). Begin with one bun in the center of the pan; then space the other 8 buns evenly around it, with the seam of each bun touching the side of the pan. There will still be space between the 8 pieces around the outside of the pan; this is fine.

(*If you are using the square pan and loaf pan, set it up this way:* 3 buns go in the loaf pan and 6 go in the square pan. Space the 3 buns evenly across the loaf pan from end to end; be sure the seam of each bun faces a side of the pan. In the square pan, you'll have 3 rows, from top to bottom, with 2 buns in each row. Place the first bun in the upper left corner and the second bun to the right, about halfway across the pan. Then stagger the middle layer under those two, placing two more buns below the spaces in the first row. End with the third layer on the bottom, positioned the same way as the first layer. There will still be some spaces between the buns; this is fine).

If using the springform pan, place it in the center of the middle rack of the oven. If using the square and loaf pans, place the square pan in the center of the top rack and the loaf pan in the center of the bottom rack. Bake for 25-30 minutes, rotating pans about halfway through, until the rolls puff up a bit and the area around the filling is lightly browned. The tops of the buns should be dry and firm. Remove from oven and allow to cool for about 5 minutes before topping with the glaze.

While the buns bake, prepare the glaze: In a small bowl, combine the Sucanat and cornstarch. Add 1-2 tablespoons (15-30 ml) of the soymilk and mix it in completely; allow the mixture to sit for 5 minutes or so to allow the Sucanat to dissolve. If the glaze is still too thick at this point, add more milk, a teaspoon (5 ml) at a time, until the glaze is pourable but still thick; you want it to run off the tops of the rolls, but it should not be so thin that it pools at the bottom of the pans.

Drizzle the rolls evenly with the glaze. Allow to cool before cutting or pulling apart. Serve straight from the pan or remove to serving plates. Makes 9 cinnamon buns. May be frozen.

> **Tip 1:** If you're out of orange juice, you may substitute plain or vanilla soy or almond milk mixed with 1 tsp (5 ml) apple cider vinegar.

> **Tip 2:** If you don't have a rolling pin, a clean, empty tall glass jar, wine bottle or even a tall glass can do the job in a pinch.

Corn Crêpes

These satisfying crêpes acquire their slight sweetness from the juicy corn kernels throughout, but they marry perfectly with a little maple syrup. They're also great for brunch with savory toppings such as tomato sauce or mushroom gravy.

3 Tbsp (45 ml) sunflower or other light-tasting oil, preferably organic

1 cup (240 ml) unsweetened soymilk or almond milk

1 tsp (5 ml) apple cider vinegar

1/2 cup (120 ml) corn kernels, freshly cooked, frozen, or canned (defrost first if frozen; drain first if canned)

1/2 cup (120 ml) water or liquid from canned corn

1 Tbsp (15 ml) finely ground flax seeds

1 Tbsp (15 ml) agave nectar, light or dark

3/4 cup (105 g) light spelt flour

3 Tbsp (45 ml) organic cornmeal

3/4 tsp (3.5 ml) baking powder

1/4 tsp (1 ml) baking soda

1/4 tsp (1 ml) fine sea salt

In a medium bowl, mix together the oil, soymilk, vinegar, corn kernels, water, flax seeds and agave nectar. Stir well and set aside while you prepare the dry ingredients, or at least 2 minutes.

In a large bowl, sift the flour, cornmeal, baking powder, soda and salt. Pour the wet mixture over the dry and stir just to blend (don't worry if a few small lumps remain here and there). The batter will be thin.

Heat a nonstick frypan over medium heat. Using a medium ice cream scoop or 1/4 cup (60 ml) measuring cup, scoop the batter and pour onto hot pan. Cook for 4-5 minutes, until bubbles appear and pop on the surface of the crêpes, and the edges look dry. Flip the crêpes and cook another 1-2 minutes. Serve immediately. May be frozen.

> **Variation:** For savory crêpes, add 1 Tbsp (15 ml) freshly chopped dill or 1 tsp (5 ml) dried dill, and 1/4 tsp (1 ml) smoked paprika along with the dry ingredients.

Fluffy Fruited Pancakes

These light and foolproof pancakes are great with berries, apples, pears, or bananas. Unlike most animal-free versions, they provide a good amount of protein on their own, due to the protein powder added to the batter. You can use leftovers for another day's breakfast or lunch: simply spread one pancake with your favorite nut butter and/or jam, then top with another pancake for a quick and delicious pancake "sandwich."

- 1-3/4 cups (420 ml) plain or vanilla soy, almond or rice milk
- 2 Tbsp (30 ml) finely ground flax seeds
- 2 tsp (10 ml) apple cider vinegar
- 3 Tbsp (45 ml) sunflower or other light-tasting oil, preferably organic
- 1 Tbsp (15 ml) agave nectar, light or dark, or maple syrup
- 1-3/4 cups (245 g) whole spelt flour
- 2 Tbsp (30 ml) unflavored protein powder (rice or soy are ideal); you may substitute soy or chickpea flour, sifted
- 1 Tbsp (15 ml) baking powder
- 1/2 tsp (2.5 ml) baking soda
- 1/4 tsp (1 ml) fine sea salt
- 1 cup (240 ml) fresh or frozen berries or chopped apple, pear or banana (do not thaw if using frozen fruit)

Measure the soy milk into a glass measuring cup or bowl and add the flax, vinegar, oil and agave nectar, stirring well. Set aside while you measure the dry ingredients, or for at least 2 minutes.

In a large bowl, sift the flour, protein powder, baking powder, baking soda and salt. Pour the wet ingredients over the dry and mix just to blend (there will still be a few lumps here and there; this is fine). Gently fold in the fruit.

Heat a nonstick frypan over medium heat (spray the pan with olive oil spray if desired). Using a large ice-cream scoop or 1/3 cup (80 ml) measuring cup, pour the batter into the pan and spread slightly with the back of the scoop.

Cook each pancake about 3-4 minutes, until puffed, golden at the edges, and little bubbles appear and pop on the surface. Flip the cakes and cook another 3-4 minutes on the other side. Serve immediately. Makes 10-12 pancakes. Refrigerate leftovers, tightly wrapped, for up to 3 days. May be frozen (may be defrosted in the toaster).

French Toast Soufflé with Summer Berries

I was looking for a fast, easy way to prepare French toast, and decided I'd just bake it in a casserole dish instead of taking time to dip and fry each piece. The result was this spectacular soufflé: light, airy, and filled with bursts of juicy berries. This dish is great for a brunch buffet or even dessert. And you won't need to wait for summer, as frozen berries work equally well here.

- **8-10 slices sourdough bread (I use spelt or kamut)**
- **1/4 cup (30 g) old-fashioned rolled oats (not instant)**
- **2-1/2 cups (600 ml) vanilla soy, almond or rice milk**
- **1 tsp (5 ml) pure vanilla extract**
- **1/2 cup (120 ml) light agave nectar**
- **1 Tbsp (15 ml) organic cornstarch or arrowroot powder**
- **2-3 Tbsp (30-45 ml) fruit liqueur (such as framboise, Grand Marnier, cherry, etc.), or apple juice**
- **1 Tbsp (15 ml) fresh lemon juice or 1/2 tsp (2.5 ml) pure lemon extract**
- **1-1/2 to 2 cups (360-480 ml) fresh or frozen berries (use one or a mixture of blueberries, raspberries, strawberries, blackberries or pitted cherries)—do not thaw if frozen**

Preheat oven to 350F (180C). Lightly grease a nonreactive (glass or ceramic) pan or soufflé dish.

Break the bread into bite-sized chunks and place in a large bowl. Set aside.

In a blender or food processor, grind the oats until they are the consistency of a coarse meal. Add the remaining ingredients except for the bread and berries and blend until smooth. Pour the mixture over the bread in the bowl, pushing the bread down with the back of a spoon so that all pieces are submerged. Allow to sit 20-30 minutes, pressing the bread back down occasionally, until the bread is completely soaked through (there may still be liquid left in the bottom of the bowl; this is fine).

When the bread is all soaked, spoon half the bread slices and half of any remaining liquid into the prepared pan. Top with about 2/3 of the mixed berries. Cover the berries with the rest of the bread and liquid, then top with the last 1/3 of the berries.

Bake in preheated oven 40-50 minutes, rotating pan about halfway through, until puffed and golden and a knife inserted in the center comes out wet but clean. Allow to cool at least 10 minutes before serving. Serve warm, at room temperature, or cold. Makes about 8 servings. This is best served the day it's made, though it can be re-heated the next day.

Variation: For a slightly different taste and texture, use chopped dried apricots, raisins, or other dried fruits in place of the berries. First cover the dried fruits with boiling water and allow to sit for about 5 minutes; then drain and add to the recipe. Use the drained liquid to replace the liqueur in the recipe if you like.

Gingered Apple Muffins

I'm not usually fond of baked apples, but diced in these muffins, they're perfect. Juicy chunks of apple and the tempting zing of ginger abound in every bite. Be sure to cut the apple small, though, unless you like your muffins crunchy.

- **2 small, crisp apples, such as Gala, Granny Smith or Empire**
- **2 tsp (10 ml) ground cinnamon**
- **1/2 cup (120 ml) packed silken tofu**
- **1/4 cup (60 ml) pure maple syrup**
- **3/4 cup (180 ml) plain or vanilla soy or almond milk**
- **1/4 cup (60 ml) sunflower or other light-tasting oil, preferably organic**
- **1/2 tsp (2.5 ml) apple cider vinegar**
- **1 cup (140 g) light spelt flour**
- **3/4 cup (100 g) whole spelt flour**
- **2 tsp (10 ml) baking powder**
- **3/4 tsp (7.5 ml) baking soda**
- **1/4 tsp (1 ml) fine sea salt**
- **1/4 cup (40 g) finely chopped candied ginger**

Preheat oven to 375F (190C). Line 9 muffin cups (or 12 muffin cups, for small muffins) with paper liners, or spray with nonstick spray.

Wash, core and dice the apples (there's no need to peel them, unless you prefer them peeled). The pieces should be fairly small (the size of large blueberries or raspberries is best) so that they will soften completely while baking. Toss with the cinnamon to coat. Set aside.

In the bowl of a food processor, blend the tofu, maple syrup, soymilk, oil and vinegar until smooth and no lumps of tofu are visible. Set aside.

In a large bowl, sift together the light spelt flour, whole spelt flour, baking powder, baking soda and salt. Add the chopped ginger and toss to distribute.

Pour the tofu mixture over the dry ingredients and stir just to blend. Fold in the apple mixture.

Using a large ice cream scoop or 1/3 cup (80ml) measuring cup, fill the muffin cups about 3/4 full (these muffins don't rise much more when baked). Bake in preheated oven 20-25 minutes, rotating the pans about halfway through, until a tester inserted in one of the center muffins comes out clean. Cool 5 minutes in pan before removing to a rack to cook completely. May be frozen.

Lemon Blueberry Scones

These are a sweeter, slightly more delicate version of tea biscuits. You can add a variety of different fruits or nuts for equally great results—see the variations, below.

1 tsp (5 ml) apple cider vinegar, plus enough soy, rice or almond milk to equal 1/2 cup (120 ml)

1/4 cup (60 ml) light agave nectar

3 Tbsp (45 ml) sunflower or other light-tasting oil, preferably organic

1 tsp (5 ml) pure vanilla extract

Finely grated zest of one lemon

1-3/4 cups (245 g) light spelt flour

1-1/2 tsp (7.5 ml) baking powder

1/2 tsp (2.5 ml) baking soda

3/4 tsp (3.5 ml) fine sea salt

1/2 cup (60 g) fresh or frozen blueberries (do not thaw first if frozen)

2 Tbsp soy, rice, or almond milk (for brushing tops), if desired

Preheat oven to 400F (200C). Line a cookie sheet with parchment paper, or spray with nonstick spray.

In a small bowl, combine the vinegar-milk mixture, agave nectar, oil and vanilla; whisk to blend well, then stir in the lemon zest. Set aside.

In a medium bowl, sift together the flour, baking powder, baking soda and salt. Pour the wet ingredients over the dry and stir to mix well; do not overmix. The dough will be thick and sticky. Carefully fold in the blueberries.

Using a large ice cream scoop or 1/3 cup (80 ml) measuring cup, drop mounds of dough onto the cookie sheet about 2 inches (5 cm) apart. Wet your hands (or use a silicon spatula) and flatten the biscuits slightly.

Bake in preheated oven for 6 minutes, then remove and quickly brush tops with 2 Tbsp (30 ml) milk, if desired (this creates a more golden crust). Rotate the pan, return to oven and bake another 6-8 minutes, until the edges are golden and tops are just beginning to brown.

Allow to cool for 5 minutes before removing to rack to cool completely. Makes 6 large biscuits. Store tightly covered or wrapped in plastic in the refrigerator up to 5 days. May be frozen.

Variations: *Orange-Pistachio Scones*: substitute orange zest for the lemon, and use 1/3 cup (80 ml) of shelled natural pistachios instead of the blueberries.

Classic Cranberry Scones: omit zest and increase vanilla to 1 Tbsp (15 ml). Use 1/2 cup (60 g) fresh or frozen (unthawed) cranberries in place of the blueberries.

Maple Millet Muffins

I got the inspiration for these muffins from the amazing Mollie Katzen, whose Sunlight Café *contains a few muffin variations with whole grains. The millet in these substantive muffins is stirred into the batter raw, then bakes up crunchy in the final product, almost like rice crisps hidden in the muffins.*

- 3-1/2 ounces (110 g) pitted dried unsweetened dates, chopped (about 25 dates, not Medjool) (see note)
- 1/3 cup (80 ml) boiling water (see note)
- 1/3 cup (80 ml) sunflower or other light-tasting oil
- 3 Tbsp (45 ml) blackstrap molasses
- 1/3 cup (80 ml) pure maple syrup
- 1 cup (240 ml) plain or vanilla soy or almond milk
- 1/4 cup (25 g) finely ground flax seeds
- 1 Tbsp (15 ml) pure vanilla extract
- 1/2 tsp (2.5 ml) apple cider vinegar
- 3/4 cup (105 g) raisins
- 2-3/4 cups (375 g) whole spelt flour
- 1 Tbsp plus 1 tsp (20 ml) baking powder
- 3/4 tsp (3.5 ml) baking soda
- 1 Tbsp (15 ml) cinnamon
- Scant 1/2 tsp (2 ml) nutmeg
- 1/2 tsp (2.5 ml) fine sea salt
- 2/3 cup (150 g) dry whole millet

Preheat oven to 350F (180C). Line 12 muffin cups with paper liners, or spray with nonstick spray.

Place the dates in a small, deep bowl and pour the boiling water over them. Cover and let soak for 5 minutes.

Purée the dates and their soaking water in a food processor until almost smooth. Add the oil, molasses, maple syrup, soymilk, flax seeds, vanilla and vinegar and process again until smooth and most of the date has been incorporated (it's okay if there are tiny flecks of date here and there, but there should be no large pieces). Add the raisins and stir by hand to coat them, but don't process again.

In a large bowl, sift together the flour, baking powder, baking soda, cinnamon, nutmeg and salt; stir to blend. Add the millet and stir to distribute it.

Pour the wet ingredients over the dry and stir to combine; do not overmix (it's okay if there are a few small dry spots here and there). Using a large ice cream scoop or 1/3 cup (80 ml) measuring cup, scoop the batter into the muffin cups, distributing it evenly (they will be quite full). Bake in preheated oven for 25-30 minutes, rotating pan about halfway through, until a tester inserted in the middle of one muffin comes out clean. Cool for 5 minutes before removing to a rack to cool completely. Makes 12 large muffins. May be frozen.

> **Note:** If you have ready-made date purée (the only ingredients should be dates and water), you can use 1/2 cup or 135 g. of the purée in place of the dates and water.

Mini Sweet Potato and Chocolate Chip Muffins

Sweet potatoes are a favorite food of mine, and I love to use them in baking as well as savory dishes. This is my adaptation of a popular recipe floating around the Internet, featuring the sweet spuds combined with chocolate for an irresistible treat.

- 1/2 cup (90 g) Sucanat (or other unrefined evaporated cane juice)
- 1/3 cup (80 ml) sunflower or other light-tasting oil, preferably organic
- 2 tsp (10 ml) finely ground flax seeds
- 2 Tbsp (30 ml) plain or vanilla soy or almond milk
- 1 tsp (5 ml) pure vanilla extract
- 1/2 cup (120 ml) packed sweet potato purée (see note)
- 1 cup (140 g) light spelt flour
- 1 tsp (5 ml) cinnamon
- 1/4 tsp (1 ml) ground ginger
- 1/8 tsp (.5 ml) ground cloves
- Pinch nutmeg
- 1/2 tsp (2.5 ml) baking soda
- 1/4 tsp (1 ml) baking powder
- 1/4 tsp (1 ml) fine sea salt
- 2/3 cup (135 g) dairy-free chocolate chips

Preheat oven to 350F (180C). Spray 18 mini muffin cups or 6 regular cups with nonstick spray, or line with miniature paper liners.

In a large bowl, mix together the Sucanat, oil, flax, milk, vanilla and sweet potato; stir to combine well. Set aside while you measure the dry ingredients, or at least 2 minutes.

In a medium bowl, sift together the flour, cinnamon, ginger, cloves, nutmeg, baking soda, baking powder and salt. Pour the wet ingredients over the dry and stir to combine. Gently stir in the chocolate chips.

Using a small ice cream scoop or tablespoon (15 ml), scoop the batter and fill the muffin cups about 3/4 full. Bake in preheated oven for 15-20 minutes (25-30 for regular sized muffins), rotating pans about halfway through, until a tester inserted in a center muffin comes out clean. Cool completely and remove from tins. Makes about 18 mini muffins. May be frozen.

Note: To make your own purée, boil or bake sweet potatoes until soft and then whir the flesh in a food processor until smooth. If using canned purée, check that the only ingredient is cooked sweet potatoes.

Multi-Seed Muffins

I wanted to make a muffin that showcased all the healthy seeds that I love to eat, all in one place. These were a favorite of mine when I sold them at an organic market in the Toronto area. The five spice powder provides just a hint of spice without being too bold in this moist and substantial muffin.

- 3-1/2 ounces (110 g) pitted dried unsweetened dates, chopped (about 25 dates, not Medjool) (see note)
- 1/3 cup (80 ml) boiling water (see note)
- 3/4 cup (180 ml) plain or vanilla soy or almond milk
- 1/4 cup (25 g) finely ground flax seeds
- 1/3 cup (80 ml) sunflower or other light-tasting oil, preferably organic
- 1/2 cup plus 2 Tbsp (150 ml) pure maple syrup
- 1 tsp (5 ml) pure vanilla extract
- 1/4 tsp (1 ml) apple cider vinegar
- 1/2 cup (75 g) coarsely chopped, lightly toasted natural cashews
- 2 Tbsp (30 ml) poppyseeds
- 1/4 cup (35 g) whole flax seeds
- 1/4 cup (35 g) raw or toasted sesame seeds
- 1/4 cup (35 g) raw or toasted pumpkin seeds
- 1/4 cup (35 g) raw or toasted sunflower seeds
- 1-1/3 cups (170 g) whole spelt flour
- 1-1/2 cups (215 g) light spelt flour
- 1 Tbsp (15 ml) baking powder
- 1 tsp (5 ml) baking soda
- 1/4 tsp (1 ml) fine sea salt
- 3/4 tsp (7.5 ml) Chinese five spice powder; or use 1/2 tsp (2.5 ml) cinnamon plus 1/8 tsp (.5 ml) cardamom

Preheat oven to 350F (180C). Line 12 muffin cups with paper liners, or spray with nonstick spray.

Place dates in a small bowl and pour the boiling water over them. Allow to soak for 5 minutes, then transfer the mixture (both dates and water) to the bowl of a food processor. Process until smooth.

To the processor, add the milk, ground flax seeds, oil, maple syrup, vanilla and apple cider vinegar; process again until mixture is very smooth and no large pieces of date are visible. Add the cashews, poppyseeds, whole flax seeds, sesame seeds, pumpkin seeds and sunflower seeds, and stir with a spatula until seeds are covered with the mixture; do not process again. Set aside while you measure the dry ingredients, or at least 2 minutes.

In a large bowl, sift the whole spelt flour, light spelt flour, baking powder, baking soda, salt and Chinese five spice powder. Pour the wet mixture over the dry and stir just to blend; it's okay if a few small dry spots remain here and there.

Using a large ice cream scoop or 1/3 cup (80 ml) measuring cup, scoop the batter and fill the muffin cups, dividing it evenly. The cups will be very full (if you prefer smaller muffins, you can make 14 muffins instead of 12).

Bake in preheated oven for 35-40 minutes, rotating pan about halfway through, until a tester inserted in one of the center muffins comes out clean. Cool for 5 minutes before removing to a rack to cool completely. Makes 12 large or 14 smaller muffins. May be frozen.

> **Note:** If you have ready-made date purée (the only ingredients should be dates and water), you can use 1/2 cup or 135 g. of the purée in place of the dates and water.

Oatbran Banana Muffins

Not too sweet yet moist and flavorful, these muffins provide ample fiber with heart-healthy oatbran. Bananas, high in potassium, can also help maintain cardiovascular health. But the great taste is why you'll want to eat these!

> **2 cups (16-1/2 ounces or 475 g) banana purée, from about 4 medium very ripe bananas (fresh or frozen)**
>
> **1/4 cup (25 g) finely ground flax seeds**
>
> **1/3 cup (80 ml) light agave nectar**
>
> **1/2 cup (120 ml) sunflower or other light-tasting oil, preferably organic**
>
> **1-1/2 tsp (7.5 ml) pure vanilla extract**
>
> **1/4 tsp (1 ml) apple cider vinegar**
>
> **1/2 cup (70 g) raisins**
>
> **1-3/4 cups plus 2 Tbsp (250 g) whole spelt flour**
>
> **1-1/2 tsp (7.5 ml) baking soda**
>
> **2 tsp (10 ml) baking powder**
>
> **1/4 tsp (1 ml) fine sea salt**
>
> **1-1/2 cups (185 g) oat bran**

Preheat oven to 350F (180C). Line 12 muffin cups with paper liners, or spray with nonstick spray.

In a large bowl, whisk together the banana purée, flax seeds, agave nectar, oil, vanilla and vinegar. Add the raisins and stir to coat. Set aside while you measure the dry ingredients, or at least 2 minutes.

In a large bowl, sift together the flour, baking soda, baking powder and salt. Add the oat bran and stir to combine.

Pour the wet mixture over the dry and stir to blend well (it's okay if a few dry spots remain here and there). Using a large ice cream scoop or 1/3 cup (80 ml) measuring cup, scoop the batter into the muffin tins, dividing it equally among the 12 cups (they will be very full).

Bake in preheated oven for 25-30 minutes, rotating pan about halfway through, until tops are deep golden brown and a tester inserted in a center muffin comes out clean. Cool for 5 minutes in pan, then remove to a rack to cool completely. Makes 12 large muffins. May be frozen.

Tip: You can use either fresh or frozen bananas for this recipe; if using frozen, simply defrost in the bowl of the food processor or blender, then whir to make your own purée.

Oatmeal Walnut Scones

These are a great treat to make with leftover oatmeal from yesterday's breakfast. The oats add chewiness, and the walnuts provide healthy Omega 3 fats. We like these so much in our house that I make extra oatmeal in the morning so I'll have enough left over for the scones!

- **2/3 cup (160 ml) cooked steel-cut oats (cooked rolled oats are not suitable for this recipe)**
- **1/4 cup (60 ml) agave nectar, light or dark**
- **2/3 cup (160 ml) plain or vanilla soy or almond milk**
- **1 tsp (5 ml) apple cider vinegar**
- **3 Tbsp (45 ml) sunflower or other light-tasting oil, preferably organic**
- **1 tsp (5 ml) pure vanilla extract**
- **1/3 cup (40 g) chopped walnuts, lightly toasted**
- **1-1/3 cups (185 g) light spelt flour**
- **2-1/2 tsp (12.5 ml) aluminum-free baking powder**
- **1/2 tsp (2.5 ml) baking soda**
- **3/4 tsp (3.5 ml) fine sea salt**
- **1-1/2 tsp (7.5 ml) cinnamon**
- **Extra soymilk (about 1/3 cup or 80 ml) for brushing tops**

Preheat oven to 375F (190C). Line two cookie sheets with parchment paper, or spray with nonstick spray.

In a medium bowl, combine the oats, agave nectar, soymilk, vinegar, oil and vanilla. Mix well, then gently stir in the walnuts. Set aside.

In a large bowl, sift together the flour, baking powder, baking soda, salt and cinnamon. Pour the wet mixture over the dry and stir to mix well (it will seem too soft for a scone dough; this is as it should be).

Using a large ice-cream scoop or 1/3 cup (80 ml) measuring cup, scoop dough and place 2 inches (5 cm) apart on the cookie sheet. Wet your palms and flatten the scones slightly.

Bake in preheated oven for 12 minutes, then remove the pan and quickly brush the tops with the extra soymilk, if desired. Rotate the pan and return it to the oven for another 8-10 minutes, until edges are golden and tops are firm. Makes 12 scones. May be frozen.

Orange Oat Muffins

Unlike many low-fat muffins, these taste great: they are moist and flavorful, with an intense orange presence. There's also substantial fiber from the fruits and whole spelt. Using a food processor means these are incredibly easy to prepare!

1 medium organic seedless orange, washed, whole and with skin

1 Tbsp (15 ml) finely ground flax seeds

3 Tbsp (45 ml) water

1/2 cup (60 g) finely chopped dates (they should be soft)

3 Tbsp (45 ml) sunflower or other light-tasting oil, preferably organic

1/4 cup (60 ml) pure maple syrup

2 Tbsp (30 ml) blackstrap molasses

1/2 cup (120 ml) plain or vanilla soy or almond milk

1 cup (140 g) whole spelt or kamut (145 g) flour, or a combination

1 Tbsp (15 ml) baking powder

1 tsp (5 ml) baking soda

1/4 tsp (1 ml) fine sea salt

1 cup (100 g) old-fashioned whole rolled oats (not quick-cooking or instant)

Preheat oven to 375F (190C). Line 9 muffin cups with paper liners for large muffins (or 12 cups for smaller muffins), or spray with nonstick spray.

Cut the orange into 8 sections and process in the bowl of a food processor until almost smooth. Add the flax seeds, water, dates, oil, maple syrup, molasses and soy milk and process again until smooth (it's okay if you see tiny flecks of date or orange still in the mixture, but none should be larger than sunflower seeds). Set aside while you measure the dry ingredients, or at least 2 minutes.

In a large bowl, sift the flour, baking powder, soda and salt; add the oats and mix to combine.

Pour the wet mixture over the dry and stir just until combined (it's okay if a few dry spots remain here or there). Using a large ice cream scoop or 1/3 cup (80 ml) measuring cup, spoon the batter into the prepared muffin cups (they will be quite full).

Bake in preheated oven for 15-20 minutes, rotating pan about halfway through, until a tester inserted in one of the center muffins comes out clean. Cool 5 minutes in pans before removing to a rack to cool completely. These are better the next day, as flavors develop. Makes 9 large or 12 smaller muffins. May be frozen.

Orange Raisin Tea Cakes

My mother used to buy packages of 6 tea biscuits at the supermarket, and they'd be gone from our kitchen in minutes. This is my grown-up, much more healthy version.

1 tsp (5 ml) apple cider vinegar, plus enough plain or vanilla soy or almond milk to make 2/3 cup (160 ml)

2 Tbsp (30 ml) light agave nectar

3 Tbsp (45 ml) sunflower or other light-tasting oil, preferably organic

2 tsp (10 ml) pure vanilla extract

Finely grated zest of one small orange

1/3 cup (40 g) raisins

1-3/4 cups (245 g) light spelt flour

1-1/4 tsp (6 ml) baking powder

1/2 tsp (2.5 ml) baking soda

Scant 1/2 tsp (2.5 ml) fine sea salt

Preheat oven to 400F (200C). Line a cookie sheet with parchment paper, or spray with nonstick spray.

In a small bowl, combine the vinegar-milk mixture, agave nectar, oil and vanilla; whisk to blend well, then stir in the orange zest and raisins. Set aside.

In a medium bowl, sift together the flour, baking powder, baking soda and salt. Pour the wet ingredients over the dry and stir to mix well; do not overmix. The dough will be thick and sticky.

Using a large ice cream scoop or 1/3 cup (80 ml) measuring cup, drop mounds of dough onto the cookie sheet about 2 inches (5 cm) apart. Wet your hands (or use a silicon spatula) and flatten the tea cakes slightly.

Bake in preheated oven for 6 minutes, then remove and quickly brush tops with more milk, if desired (this produces a more golden crust). Rotate the pan, return to oven and bake another 6-8 minutes, until the edges are golden and tops are just beginning to brown.

Allow to cool for 5 minutes before removing to rack to cool completely. Makes 6 tea cakes. Store tightly covered or wrapped in plastic in the refrigerator up to 5 days. May be frozen.

> **Variations:** Substitute lemon zest for the orange, and currants or chopped dates for the raisins.

PB & G Muffins

The "G" in these muffins stands for "ginger." Taking a cue from one of my favorite cuisines, Thai food, I decided to combine the flavors of peanut butter with spicy ginger (along with sweet, chewy dried cranberries). The result is a moist, flavorful and satisfying muffin.

- **5-1/4 ounces (150 g) pitted dried unsweetened dates, chopped (24-26 medium dates, not Medjool) (see note)**
- **Enough boiling water to cover the dates (see note)**
- **1/2 cup (120 ml) pure maple syrup**
- **1/2 cup (120 ml) plain or vanilla soy or almond milk**
- **2/3 cup (160 ml) packed natural smooth peanut butter**
- **1/4 cup (60 ml) sunflower or other light-tasting oil, preferably organic**
- **2 Tbsp (30 ml) finely ground flax seeds**
- **1 tsp (5 ml) pure vanilla extract**
- **1 tsp (5 ml) apple cider vinegar**
- **1/3 cup (40 g) dried cranberries**
- **1-1/4 cups (165 g) whole spelt flour**
- **1-1/4 cups (155 g) whole oat flour**
- **2 tsp (10 ml) baking powder**
- **1/2 tsp (2.5 ml) baking soda**
- **1/2 tsp (2.5 ml) fine sea salt**
- **1 tsp (5 ml) ground ginger**

Preheat oven to 350F (180C). Line 12 muffin cups with paper liners, or spray with nonstick spray.

In a small bowl, cover the dates with boiling water. Allow to sit for 10 minutes, then drain and place the dates in a food processor (discard the drained liquid, or use for other baking recipes).

Process dates until they form a paste. Add the maple syrup, soymilk, peanut butter, oil, flax seeds, vanilla and vinegar and purée until the mixture is smooth and creamy. Sprinkle the cranberries on top and stir them into the mixture by hand, but do not process again. Set aside while you measure the dry ingredients, or at least 2 minutes.

In a large bowl, sift the spelt flour, oat flour, baking powder, baking soda, salt and ginger. Pour the wet mixture over the dry and stir just to blend, taking care not to overmix (it's all right if a few small dry spots remain here and there).

Using a large ice cream scoop or 1/3 cup (80 ml) measuring cup, scoop the batter into the muffin cups, filling about 3/4 full. Bake in preheated oven for 30-35 minutes, rotating pan about halfway through, until a tester inserted in a center muffin comes out clean. Allow to cool 5 minutes before removing to a rack to cool completely. Makes 12 muffins. May be frozen.

> **Note:** If you have ready-made date purée (the only ingredients should be dates and water), you can use 1/2 cup or 135 g. of the purée in place of the dates and water.

Pear and Ginger Mini Loaves or Muffins

Wonderfully moist and tempting, these loaves feature the winning combination of pear and ginger. Unlike most recipes for pear muffins, however, this one uses a pear purée, so you can taste the fruit in every mouthful.

**1-1/3 cups (320 ml) pear purée (from about 3-4 overripe, medium pears; use
    fresh or previously frozen purée) (see note)**
2 tsp (10 ml) freshly grated ginger root
2 Tbsp (15 ml) finely ground chia seeds
2/3 cup (160 ml) agave nectar, light or dark
1/2 cup (120 ml) sunflower or other light-tasting oil, preferably organic
1 Tbsp (15 ml) balsamic vinegar
1 tsp (5 ml) pure vanilla extract
1/2 tsp (2.5 ml) pure lemon extract
2/3 cup (80 g) coarsely chopped walnuts
1-1/3 cups (170g) barley flour
2/3 cup (85 g) whole oat flour
1-1/2 tsp (7.5 ml) baking powder
1 tsp (5 ml) baking soda
1/4 tsp (1 ml) fine sea salt
2 tsp (10 ml) cinnamon
Scant 1/4 tsp (1 ml) ground cloves

Preheat oven to 350F (180C). Line 10 mini loaf pans or 10-12 muffin cups with paper liners, or spray with nonstick spray. If using individual loaf pans, place them on a cookie sheet.

In a medium bowl, combine the pear purée, ginger, chia seeds, agave nectar, oil, vinegar, vanilla and lemon extract; whisk to combine, then stir in the nuts to coat. Set aside while you measure the dry ingredients, or at least 2 minutes.

In a large bowl, sift the barley flour, oat flour, baking powder, baking soda, salt, cinnamon and cloves. Stir briefly to combine. Pour the wet mixture over the dry and stir just to blend (it's okay if a few dry spots remain here and there).

Using a large ice cream scoop or 1/3 cup (80 ml) measuring cup, pour the mixture into the pans and fill about 3/4 full (these won't rise much while baking).

Bake in preheated oven for 30-35 minutes, rotating the cookie sheet about halfway through, until loaves appear domed and dry on top, and a tester inserted in one of the center loaves comes out clean but moist.

Cool at least 5 minutes in pans before transferring to a rack to cool completely. Store tightly covered or wrapped in plastic wrap in the refrigerator for up to 5 days. Makes 8 mini loaves or 10-12 muffins. May be frozen.

> **Note**: You can make your own purée by cutting washed, cored pears into eighths and processing in a food processor or blender.

Pear and Pecan Scones

The pears in these scones add more sweetness than they do any strong pear flavor, while the rice flour provides body and a dense crumb. I love these for breakfast slathered with apple butter.

Scones:

1 cup (240 ml) pear purée (from 2 large, very ripe pears, about 8 ounces or 230 g; use fresh or previously frozen purée) (see note)

2 Tbsp (30 ml) light agave nectar

3 Tbsp (45 ml) sunflower or other light-tasting oil, preferably organic

1 Tbsp (15 ml) pure vanilla extract

1/2 tsp (2.5 ml) pure almond extract

1 tsp (5 ml) apple cider vinegar

1 Tbsp (15 ml) finely ground flax seeds

2/3 cup (75 g) coarsely chopped pecans

1-1/4 cups (180 g) light spelt flour

2/3 cup (100 g) brown rice flour

1/2 tsp (2.5 ml) Chinese five spice powder (or use cinnamon)

2 tsp (10 ml) baking powder

1/4 tsp (1 ml) baking soda

1/4 tsp (1 ml) fine sea salt

Glaze (optional):

1 Tbsp (15 ml) light agave nectar

1 Tbsp (15 ml) water

Preheat oven to 375F (190C). Line the bottom of an 8" (20 cm) round pan with parchment paper, or spray with nonstick spray.

Make the scones: In a medium bowl, combine the pear purée, agave nectar, oil, vanilla, almond extract, vinegar and flax seeds. Add the nuts and stir to coat. Set aside while you measure the dry ingredients, or at least 2 minutes.

In a large bowl, sift the spelt flour, rice flour, five spice powder, baking powder, baking soda and salt. Pour the wet mixture over the dry and stir to combine well. You will have a thick batter (it won't be as firm as a dough). Turn the mixture into the pan and spread to fill the pan evenly; smooth the top. Using a sharp knife, score the top, cutting lines about 1/8" (3 mm) deep to outline 6 pie-shaped wedges.

While the scones bake, mix the glaze: in a small bowl, combine the agave nectar and water.

Bake in preheated oven for 20 minutes. Remove from oven and brush quickly with glaze, if using. Rotate the pan and return to the oven for 10-15 more minutes, until the edges are dark golden brown and the top is browned in spots. The top of the scones should feel firm to the touch.

Allow to cool in pan before cutting along the lines into 6 scones. May be frozen.

> **Note**: You can make your own purée by cutting washed, cored pears into eighths and processing in a food processor or blender.

Plum Good Oaty Pancakes

While the plums in these pancakes provide a wonderful juiciness and tang, you could easily substitute sliced peaches or even apples. And they're a great way to consume your oatmeal and pancakes in one dish!

1/2 cup (50 g) whole old-fashioned oats (not quick-cooking or instant)

1 Tbsp (15 ml) finely ground chia seeds

1-1/2 cups (360 ml) plain or vanilla almond or soy milk

2 Tbsp (30 ml) light agave nectar

1 Tbsp (15 ml) sunflower or other light-tasting oil, preferably organic

1/2 tsp (2.5 ml) pure lemon flavoring or 2 tsp grated lemon zest

3-4 small ripe red plums, pit removed and sliced into thin half-moons

2/3 cup (90 g) light spelt flour

2/3 cup (80 g) barley flour

2 tsp (10 ml) baking powder

1/8 tsp (1 ml) fine sea salt

In a medium bowl, combine the oats, chia seeds, milk, agave nectar, oil and lemon flavoring; whisk well to blend and to ensure there are no lumps of ground chia seeds visible. Stir in the plum slices. Set aside for at least 20 minutes.

Meanwhile, in a large bowl, sift together the spelt flour, barley flour, baking powder and salt.

Heat a large frypan over medium heat (if it's not a nonstick pan, spray lightly with oil or nonstick spray). Stir the wet mixture to eliminate any lumps, then pour the wet mixture over the dry and stir just to blend.

Using a large ice cream scoop or 1/3 cup (80 ml) measuring cup, scoop the batter into pan the pan and spread to flatten slightly. Allow to cook about 4-5 minutes until edges are dry and small bubbles appear and pop on top of the pancakes. Flip and cook the other side for another 3-4 minutes, until golden. Keep warm until all pancakes are cooked; serve immediately with maple syrup or jam of your choice. Makes 8-10 pancakes. May be frozen.

Poppyseed Soda Bread

This bread is incredibly versatile and easy: you can shape the dough into a large round and bake it on a cookie sheet, or place it in a loaf pan for a tall, tender loaf. Great for sandwiches, jam, or snacking, this bread is moist and light, and keeps beautifully for a few days.

- **1 package (12 oz. or 375 g) aseptically-packaged firm silken tofu (such as Mori-Nu) (see note)**
- **3/4 cup (180 ml) water, room temperature**
- **2 tsp (10 ml) apple cider vinegar**
- **1/4 cup (45 g) Sucanat (or other unrefined evaporated cane juice)**
- **1/3 cup (80 ml) sunflower or other light-tasting oil, preferably organic**
- **2 Tbsp (30 ml) poppyseeds**
- **3-1/2 cups (500 g) light spelt flour, plus more for kneading**
- **2 tsp (10 ml) baking powder**
- **1-1/2 tsp (7.5 ml) baking soda**
- **1 tsp (5 ml) fine sea salt**
- **About 1/4 cup (60 ml) plain or unsweetened soy, almond or rice milk, for brushing tops (optional)**

Preheat oven to 350F (180C). Line two cookie sheets, two 8" (20 cm) loaf pans, or one cookie sheet and one loaf pan with parchment paper, or spray with nonstick spray.

In the bowl of a food processor, process the tofu until smooth. Add the water, vinegar, Sucanat and oil and process again, scraping down sides and ensuring no little lumps of tofu remain. Stir in poppyseeds, but do not process again.

In a large bowl, sift together the flour, baking powder, baking soda and salt. Pour the wet mixture over the dry and stir to combine (use your hands if necessary) to create a very soft, sticky dough that barely holds its shape (it should be softer than regular bread dough). Sprinkle about 1/4 cup (60 ml) flour over top of the ball of dough in the bowl, and use your hands to cut the dough in half, then form each half into a loose ball (use the flour to prevent the dough from sticking to your hands). At this point, resist the urge to add extra flour; too much will make the bread tough.

Place each ball on a cookie sheet or in a loaf pan (or one of each). For a round, freeform loaf on the cookie sheet, shape as best you can into a mound that's round and domed on top (it may begin to spread a little bit, but it should still hold a shape). Use a sharp knife to slash the top of each loaf about 1/8" (2 mm) deep two or three times across.

Bake the bread in preheated oven for 25 minutes. Remove from oven and quickly brush the tops with the extra 1/4 cup (60 ml) soymilk. Rotate pans and return to oven for another 20-25 minutes, until the top of each loaf is brown and dry. You can try tapping on the bread to see if it sounds hollow; if it does, it's definitely ready (or peek at the bottom of each loaf; if it's deep, golden brown, it's ready).

Allow to cool in pan 5 minutes before removing to a cooling rack. This is especially delicious warm. Store in an airtight container or plastic wrap in refrigerator up to 5 days; bring to room temperature before eating. Makes 2 loaves. May be frozen.

> **Note**: If you have another use for half a box of tofu (such as a half recipe of Mock Chocolate Pudding, page 156), this recipe also works well halved.

Raisin Spice Tea Bread

I first started making this loaf around Christmas time because it suggested holiday festivities with its spices and raisins, but became so enamored I now make it all year round. A moist, fruity and fragrant loaf, it's equally delicious with almond butter for breakfast or with a steaming cup of tea for dessert.

- **1/2 cup (120 ml) packed coconut oil, preferably organic**
- **1-1/2 cups (360 ml) hot brewed dark tea (Earl Grey, Orange Pekoe, etc.)**
- **1 cup (140 g) raisins, dried cranberries, or a combination**
- **2 Tbsp (30 ml) finely ground flax seeds**
- **1/2 cup (120 ml) pure maple syrup**
- **1 Tbsp (15 ml) blackstrap molasses**
- **1/2 tsp (2.5 ml) apple cider vinegar**
- **2-3/4 cups (370 g) whole spelt flour**
- **2 tsp (10 ml) baking powder**
- **1/2 tsp (2.5 ml) baking soda**
- **2 tsp (10 ml) cinnamon**
- **1/2 tsp (2.5 ml) ground nutmeg**
- **1/2 tsp (2.5 ml) ground allspice**
- **1/4 tsp (1 ml) ground cloves**
- **1/4 tsp (1 ml) fine sea salt**

Preheat oven to 350F (180C). Line an 8" (20 cm) loaf pan with parchment paper, or spray with nonstick spray.

Place the coconut oil in a medium bowl; break into small pieces if it is solid. Pour the hot tea over the oil and stir until the oil is melted.

Add the raisins, flax seeds, maple syrup, molasses and vinegar to the bowl and stir to mix well. Allow to cool while you measure the dry ingredients, or at least 10 minutes, stirring occasionally.

In a large bowl, sift together the flour, baking powder, baking soda, cinnamon, nutmeg, allspice, cloves and salt. Whisk or stir briefly with a fork to distribute the spices.

Pour the wet mixture over the dry and stir just to blend (it's okay if a few dry spots remain here and there)—do not overmix! The mixture may begin to fizz and bubble slightly; this is fine. Pour the mixture into the loaf pan and smooth the top.

Place the pan on a cookie sheet (to catch any overflow, depending on the size of the pan) and bake one hour to 65 minutes, rotating the loaf pan about halfway through, until a tester inserted in the center comes out clean. Cool completely before removing from the pan and cutting into slices (the bread is fragile when warm, but will firm up as it cools). Makes 8-12 slices. May be frozen.

Rice and Spice Apple Pancakes

A great way to use up leftover cooked rice. The combination of apple chunks with soft, chewy grains of rice and a touch of spice makes a perfect breakfast base.

> **1 cup (240 ml) cooked rice (I use brown basmati)**
> **3/4 cup (180 ml) plain or vanilla almond, rice or soy milk**
> **1/2 tsp (2.5 ml) apple cider vinegar**
> **1 Tbsp (15 ml) finely ground flax seeds**
> **2 Tbsp (30 ml) sunflower or other light-tasting oil, preferably organic**
> **1 Tbsp (15 ml) agave nectar, light or dark**
> **1/2 medium apple, cored and cut in small cubes about 1/2 inch (1 cm) big**
> **1 cup (140 g) light spelt flour**
> **2 tsp (10 ml) baking powder**
> **1 tsp (5 ml) cinnamon**
> **1/2 tsp (2.5 ml) ground ginger**
> **Pinch cloves**
> **1/8 tsp (.5 ml) fine sea salt**

In a medium bowl, combine the rice, milk, vinegar, flax seeds, oil, agave nectar and apple. Set aside while you measure the dry ingredients, or at least 2 minutes.

In a large bowl, sift the flour, baking powder, cinnamon and salt. Pour the wet ingredients over the dry and stir just to combine (it's okay if there are a few small lumps here and there).

Using a large ice cream scoop or 1/3 cup (80 ml) measuring cup, pour the batter onto a heated nonstick frypan and cook for about 4 minutes per side, until bubbles have popped on the surface of the pancakes. Flip the pancakes and cook for 3-4 minutes on the other side. Enjoy immediately. Makes 8-10 pancakes. May be frozen.

Spiced Squash and Cornmeal Muffins

Squash adds some excellent fiber and vitamins, while cornmeal provides texture in these moist muffins. A great way to use extra cooked squash or pumpkin!

3/4 cup (180 ml) mashed, cooked squash or pumpkin purée, fresh or frozen

3/4 cup (180 ml) plain or vanilla soy or almond milk

1/3 cup (80 ml) pure maple syrup

1/4 cup (60 ml) sunflower or other light-tasting oil, preferably organic

2 tsp (10 ml) finely ground chia seeds

1 tsp (5 ml) apple cider vinegar

1/2 cup chopped pecans (50 g) or walnuts (55 g)

1-1/4 cups (170 g) whole spelt flour

1 tsp (5 ml) ground ginger

2 tsp (10 ml) cinnamon

1/2 tsp (2.5 ml) baking soda

2 tsp (10 ml) baking powder

1/4 tsp (1 ml) fine sea salt

1/2 cup (90 g) organic cornmeal

Preheat oven to 350F (180C). Line 12 muffin cups with paper liners, or spray with nonstick spray.

In a medium bowl, whisk together the squash purée, soymilk, maple syrup, oil, chia and vinegar until well combined. Add the pecans and stir to coat with the mixture. Set aside while you measure the dry ingredients, or at least 2 minutes.

In a large bowl, sift together the flour, ginger, cinnamon, baking soda, baking powder and salt. Add the cornmeal and stir well.

Pour the wet mixture over the dry and stir just to combine (it's okay if a few dry spots remain here and there). Using a large ice cream scoop or 1/3 cup (80 ml) measuring cup, scoop the batter to fill the cups evenly. Bake in preheated oven 25-30 minutes, rotating pan about halfway through, until a tester inserted in a center muffin comes out clean. Makes 12 large muffins. May be frozen.

Sunshine Breakfast Loaf

You don't taste the prunes in this moist and filling loaf, but they do add extra sweetness and fiber to the bread. They're also a source of boron, a trace mineral that's often low in people's diets and can help to keep bones healthy.

- **3-1/4 ounces (90 g) pitted prunes (7-8 large prunes; they should be soft)**
- **3/4 cup (180 ml) packed pumpkin purée (not pie filling)**
- **1/2 cup (120 ml) pure maple syrup**
- **1/2 cup (120 ml) pure orange juice**
- **1/4 cup (60 ml) sunflower or other light-tasting oil, preferably organic**
- **2 tsp (10 ml) finely ground chia seeds**
- **1 tsp (5 ml) pure vanilla extract**
- **1 tsp (5 ml) apple cider vinegar**
- **1/4 cup (35 g) unsalted pumpkin seeds, lightly toasted**
- **1/2 cup (50 g) unsalted walnut pieces, lightly toasted**
- **1-3/4 cups (240 g) whole spelt flour**
- **2 tsp (10 ml) baking powder**
- **1 tsp (5 ml) baking soda**
- **1/2 tsp (2.5 ml) fine sea salt**
- **2 tsp (5 ml) cinnamon**

Preheat oven to 350F (180C). Line an 8" (20 cm) loaf pan with parchment paper, or spray with nonstick spray.

In the bowl of a food processor, process the prunes until almost smooth. Add the pumpkin, maple syrup, orange juice, oil, chia seeds, vanilla and vinegar and process again until the mixture is well blended (it's okay if there are some small flecks of prune visible, but there should be no large pieces). Pour the pumpkin seeds and walnuts over the wet mixture and stir in by hand, but don't process again. Set aside.

In a large bowl, sift the flour, baking powder, baking soda, salt and cinnamon. Pour the wet mixture over the dry and stir just until combined (don't worry if there are a few dry spots here and there). The batter will be thick.

Turn the mixture into the prepared pan and smooth the top. Bake in preheated oven for 50 to 60 minutes, rotating pan about halfway through, until a tester comes out clean when inserted in the center of the bread and the top and sides are browned. Allow to cool in pan at least 10 minutes before turning onto a rack to cool completely. Makes 8-10 slices. May be frozen.

Sweet Harvest Muffins

This is the very first recipe I created for my company, Bake It Healthy, and it became the number one best-selling product. With a light, moist texture, and fragrant, elusive flavor reminiscent of chocolate, this muffin will please everyone. And don't forget the nutritional bonus: each muffin offers up a serving of vegetables!

- **4.5 ounces (125 g) fresh or frozen spinach (include leaves and stems)**
- **1/2 cup plus 2 Tbsp (150 ml) water**
- **1 Tbsp (15 ml) finely ground flax seeds**
- **1/3 cup (80 ml) agave nectar, light or dark**
- **1/4 cup (60 ml) blackstrap molasses**
- **1/3 cup (80 ml) sunflower or other light-tasting oil, preferably organic**
- **1/2 tsp (2.5 ml) apple cider vinegar**
- **4-1/4 ounces or 115 g (about one cup UNpacked) finely grated zucchini with skin**
- **3.5 ounces or 95 g (about one cup UNpacked) finely grated carrot**
- **1/2 cup (70 g) raisins**
- **1/2 cup (100 g) dark chocolate chips**
- **1-3/4 cups (250 g) light spelt flour**
- **3/4 cup (95 g) whole oat flour**
- **1/4 cup (30 g) carob flour or powder**
- **Heaping 1 tsp (5 ml) cinnamon**
- **1/2 tsp (2.5 ml) ground ginger**
- **2-1/2 tsp (12.5 ml) baking powder**
- **1-1/4 tsp (6 ml) baking soda**
- **1/4 tsp (1 ml) fine sea salt**

Preheat oven to 350 F (180 C). Line 12 muffin cups with paper liners, or spray with nonstick spray.

In the bowl of a food processor, whir the spinach for about 30 seconds to break it up. Add the water and flax seeds, and whir until smooth. It's all right if there are still very small specks of spinach (no larger than a sesame seed), but there should be no larger pieces visible. Add the agave nectar, molasses, oil and vinegar, and blend again. Place the grated zucchini, grated carrot, raisins and chips in the processor bowl and stir in by hand, but do not blend again. Set aside while you prepare the dry ingredients, or at least 2 minutes.

In a large bowl, sift the spelt flour, oat flour, carob powder, cinnamon, ginger, baking powder, baking soda and salt. Stir to distribute the spices evenly. Pour the wet mixture over the dry and stir just to blend—do not overmix (the mixture may begin to fizz and bubble a little; this is fine). The batter will be thick. Using a large ice cream scoop or 1/3 cup (80 ml) measuring cup, scoop the mixture into the muffin cups (they will be very full).

Bake in preheated oven for 25-30 minutes, rotating pan about halfway through, until a tester inserted in one of the center muffins comes out clean. Cool in pan for 5 minutes before removing to a cooling rack. Cool completely before tasting (the spinach flavor may be noticeable in a warm muffin but disappears once cooled). Makes 12 large muffins. May be frozen.

Sweet Potato and Cranberry Muffins

I love sweet potatoes in any form, but especially in baked goods. These muffins are incredibly light and moist, with the slight tang of orange zest. Great at the holidays when you have extra cranberries—but you'll want to make these all year.

- **1/2 cup (130 g) sweet potato purée (see tip)**
- **1/3 cup (80 ml) agave nectar, light or dark**
- **2 tsp (10 ml) finely ground chia seeds**
- **1/4 cup (60 ml) sunflower or other light-tasting oil**
- **1 Tbsp (15 ml) finely grated orange zest**
- **1/4 cup (60 ml) plain or vanilla soy or almond milk, or orange juice**
- **1/2 cup (60 g) fresh or 1/3 cup (40 g) dried cranberries**
- **1-1/2 cups (190 g) light spelt flour**
- **1 Tbsp (15 ml) baking powder**
- **1/2 tsp (2.5 ml) baking soda**
- **1 tsp (5 ml) cinnamon**
- **1/2 tsp (2.5 ml) ground nutmeg**
- **1/8 tsp (.5 ml) fine sea salt**

Preheat oven to 350F (180 C). Line a 6 muffin cups with paper liners, or spray with nonstick spray.

In a medium bowl, combine the sweet potato, agave nectar, chia seeds, oil, orange zest and milk or juice; whisk to blend well and ensure there are no little lumps of chia visible. Stir in cranberries to coat. Set aside while you prepare the dry ingredients, or at least 2 minutes.

In a large bowl, sift the flour, baking powder, baking soda, cinnamon, nutmeg and salt. Pour the wet mixture over the dry and stir to blend well, but don't overmix (it's okay if a few dry spots remain here and there).

Using a large ice cream scoop or 1/3 cup (80 ml) measuring cup, fill the muffin cups 3/4 full. Bake in preheated oven 25-30 minutes, rotating pan about halfway through, until tops are just beginning to brown and a tester inserted in one of the center muffins comes out clean. Cool 5 minutes in pan before removing to a rack to cool completely. Makes 6 muffins. May be frozen.

> **Tip:** To make your own purée, boil or bake sweet potatoes until soft and then whir the flesh in a food processor until smooth. If using canned purée, check that the only ingredient is cooked sweet potatoes.

Tropical Lemon Coconut Muffins

Combining zesty lemon with coconut in these muffins creates a spectacular breakfast treat. Puréed avocado (not detectable in the flavor) provides healthy monounsaturated fats and moistness, so you don't need any other oil. And don't worry: the Day-Glo green of the raw avocado softens when baked, leaving only a deep, lemony yellow.

1/2 cup (120 ml) packed puréed avocado flesh (about 1 large)

1/2 cup (120 ml) agave nectar, light or dark

1/4 cup (60 ml) fresh lemon juice (about 1 lemon)

2 tsp (10 ml) lemon zest (about 1 lemon)

3/4 cup (90 g) barley flour

1/2 cup (60 g) whole oat flour

1 tsp (5 ml) baking powder

3/4 tsp (7.5 ml) baking soda

1/4 tsp (1 ml) fine sea salt

1 cup (80 g) shredded unsweetened coconut

Preheat oven to 350F (180C). Line 6 muffin cups with paper liners, or spray with nonstick spray.

In a small bowl, combine the avocado purée, agave nectar, lemon juice and lemon zest. Mix until smooth and evenly blended.

In a medium bowl, sift together the barley flour, oat flour, baking powder, baking soda and salt. Stir in the coconut.

Pour the wet mixture over the dry and stir quickly to blend. (It will begin to fizz and bubble; this is as it should be). Using a large ice cream scoop or 1/3 cup (80 ml) measuring cup, fill the muffin cups about 3/4 full (they will not rise very much more during baking).

Bake in preheated oven for 20-25 minutes, rotating pan halfway through, until a tester inserted in one of the center muffins comes out clean. Cool for 5 minutes in the pan before removing from cups to cooling rack. Makes 6 large muffins. May be frozen.

Zucchini and Pineapple Mini Loaves or Muffins

CF NF SF

A healthy, hearty version of a heavier standard, this bread mixes up easily and is a great recipe for using up leftover zucchini, pineapple, or overripe avocado.

- **5 ounces (150 g) finely grated zucchini, fresh or previously frozen (about 1-1/4 cups or 300 ml)**
- **1/4 cup (60 ml) avocado purée (from about 1/2 small avocado)**
- **1/2 cup (120 ml or 100-120 g) very well-drained crushed pineapple (drain first, then measure)**
- **1/2 cup (90 g) Sucanat (or other unrefined evaporated cane juice)**
- **1/4 cup (60 ml) pure maple syrup**
- **2 Tbsp (30 ml) finely ground flax seeds**
- **2 Tbsp (30 ml) sunflower or other light-tasting oil**
- **1/2 tsp (2.5 ml) apple cider vinegar**
- **1 tsp (5 ml) pure vanilla extract**
- **Generous 1/4 cup (35-40 g) chopped dried dates**
- **3/4 cup plus 2 Tbsp (130 g) light spelt flour**
- **3/4 cup (90 g) barley flour**
- **1 tsp (5 ml) baking powder**
- **1 tsp (5 ml) baking soda**
- **1/4 tsp (1 ml) fine sea salt**
- **2 tsp (10 ml) cinnamon**

Preheat oven to 350F (180C). Line 8 mini-loaf pans or 10 muffin cups with paper liners, or spray with nonstick spray. If using individual loaf pans, place them on a cookie sheet.

In a medium bowl, combine the zucchini, avocado, pineapple, Sucanat, maple syrup, flax, oil, apple cider vinegar, vanilla and chopped dates. Stir to mix well. Set aside while you prepare the dry ingredients, or at least 2 minutes.

In a large bowl, sift together the spelt flour, barley flour, baking powder, baking soda, salt and cinnamon. Stir to distribute the leaveners and cinnamon throughout.

Pour the wet mixture over the dry and stir just to blend (don't worry if a few dry spots remain here and there). Using a large ice cream scoop or 1/3 cup (80 ml) measuring cup, fill each pan about 3/4 full.

Bake for 25-30 minutes, rotating the cookie sheet about halfway through, until a tester inserted in a center loaf comes out clean. Allow to cool in pans for about 10 minutes before removing to a cooling rack. Makes 8 loaves or 10 muffins. Store in airtight container in the refrigerator for up to 5 days (these taste even better the next day). May be frozen.

COOKIES,

BARS

and SQUARES

Ginger Coconut Cookies

recipe, page 88

Chocolate Chip Cookies

recipe, page 77

Cinnamon Coffee

Toffee Bars

recipe, page 81

Cookies, Bars and Squares

Remember the first time you baked cookies? The summer I was six, my father's great aunt came to visit and taught me how to bake chocolate chip cookies. By that time, I'd already watched my mother bake cookies countless times; my two sisters and I would sit, entranced, as Mom carefully measured the ingredients, stirred the batter in the bowl, and scooped the soft, puffy mounds, placing them on cookie sheets. Then we'd argue over who got the spatula, who got the wooden spoon, and who got the main prize—the bowl. My older sister would always win, scraping along the curved edges with a tablespoon, savoring the sweet bounty.

Once I learned how to bake, I was thrilled to be able to lick the bowl clean by myself. That season, I baked chocolate chip cookies more than 2 dozen times; and each time, I relished the batter in great spoonfuls after mixing it up (and even before scooping it onto the baking sheet!) I've since expanded my cookie repertoire, but I think chocolate chip will always remain my favorite.

In this chapter, you'll find my latest version of those archetypal cookies, as well as more modern variations such as Chocolate Mint Chocolate Chip Cookies and gluten free Cashew Chocolate Chip Cookies. Other drop cookies include moist, chewy Coconut Macaroons, Seed Jumble Cookies with their assortment of dried fruits and seeds, and Classic Peanut Butter Cookies with their characteristic grid pattern. There are even rolled Sugar-free Sugar Cookies for your holiday baking.

As for bars, you'll find three types of brownies (gluten free Amazing Bean Brownies, Dalmatian Cheesecake Brownies and Ultra Fudgy Brownies), as well as Butterscotch Blondies with Dried Cherries, a quick and easy fig bar, and sensational Cinnamon Coffee Toffee Bars.

And please, feel free to lick the bowl once you're done!

Amazing Bean Brownies

There are several bean brownie recipes on the Internet, but when I created these, I'd never come across another gluten-free version. These brownies are moist, dense, and fudgy, with the added bonus of fiber from the white beans. Don't worry: you won't be able to tell the beans are in them after they're baked!

2 cups (480 ml) very well cooked, drained white or navy beans (I use dried beans, soaked overnight, then drained and cooked; if using canned beans, rinse well with water and drain very well before measuring).

1/2 cup (120 ml) chocolate or vanilla soy or almond milk

2 Tbsp (30 ml) tahini (sesame paste)

1/3 cup (80 ml) sunflower or other light-tasting oil, preferably organic

2 Tbsp (30 ml) finely ground chia seeds

2 Tbsp (30 ml) (yes, that much!) pure vanilla extract

1 tsp (5 ml) tamari or soy sauce (this adds depth of flavor) (see note)

1 cup (180 g) Sucanat (or other unrefined evaporated cane juice)

1/4 cup (60 ml) pure maple syrup

1/2 cup (70 g) sorghum flour

1/2 cup (70 g) dark cocoa powder (preferably not Dutch process)

1-1/2 tsp (7.5 ml) baking powder (see note)

1-1/2 tsp (7.5 ml) baking soda

1/2 tsp (2.5 ml) fine sea salt

1/2 cup (100 g) chocolate chips (see note)

Preheat oven to 350F (180C). Line a 9" (22.5 cm) square pan with parchment paper, or spray with nonstick spray.

In a powerful blender (**a food processor is not suitable for this recipe**), blend the beans and soy milk until you have a very smooth purée. Add the tahini, oil, chia seeds, vanilla, soy sauce, Sucanat and maple syrup and blend again, scraping down sides as necessary, until you have a perfectly smooth, velvety purée with not even a trace of graininess or grit (this may take some patience—you may need to scrape down the sides up to 15 times, depending on the style and strength of your blender—up to 10 minutes). Set aside while you measure the dry ingredients.

In a large bowl, sift together the sorghum flour, cocoa, baking powder, baking soda and salt. Add the wet mixture to the dry and top with the chocolate chips. Stir until well combined (the batter should be quite thick). Spread the batter evenly in the prepared pan and smooth the top.

Bake in preheated oven for 55-65 minutes, rotating pan about halfway through, until a tester inserted in the center comes out moist but clean (it may have one or two crumbs still clinging to it). Remove from oven and cool completely before cutting. It's helpful to cool the brownies in the refrigerator before cutting; they will crumble apart if you try to cut them while still warm.

Makes 9 large or 12 more reasonable pieces. Store, covered, up to four days in the refrigerator. May be frozen.

> **Note:** for entirely gluten-free brownies, use GF brands of baking powder, soy sauce and chocolate chips.

> **Variation:** Make mini, two-bite brownies by baking the batter in mini muffin tins for 10-15 minutes.

Almond Butter Spice Cookies

These are a great cookie for making with kids; they'll love that they have to use their hands to mix the dough! This big-batch cookie provides a great use for my favorite nut butter.

1/2 cup (125 ml) natural smooth almond butter

1/3 cup (80 ml) sunflower or other light-tasting oil, preferably organic

1/2 cup (125 ml) packed silken tofu

1 cup (180 g) Sucanat (or other unrefined evaporated cane juice)

1 Tbsp (15 ml) blackstrap molasses

1 tsp (5 ml) pure vanilla extract

1/4 cup (60 ml) plain or vanilla soy or almond milk

2/3 cup (80 g) dried cranberries, raisins or currants

2-2/3 cups (360 g) whole spelt flour

1 tsp (5 ml) cinnamon

1-1/2 tsp (7.5 ml) baking soda

1/2 tsp (2.5 ml) baking powder

1/4 tsp (1 ml) fine sea salt

1/2 cup (55 g) old-fashioned rolled oats (not instant)

Preheat oven to 350F (180C). Line 2 cookie sheets with parchment paper, or spray with nonstick spray.

In the bowl of a food processor, process the almond butter, oil, tofu, Sucanat, molasses, vanilla and soymilk until perfectly smooth and no flecks of tofu are visible. Top with the cranberries and stir them in by hand, but do not process again. Set aside.

In a large bowl, sift the flour, cinnamon, baking soda, baking powder and salt. Add the oats and stir to blend.

Pour the wet mixture over the dry and mix together well, using your hands if necessary, until you have a firm but still pliable dough.

Using a small ice cream scoop or heaping tablespoon (15 ml), place mounds of dough about 1 inch (2.5 cm) apart on cookie sheets. Flatten each cookie slightly with your palm or the bottom of a glass. (For a more decorative finish, dip the glass in Sucanat before flattening each cookie.)

Bake 12-15 minutes, rotating sheets about halfway through, until cookies are browned on the edges. Cool 5 minutes before removing from sheets. Makes about 36 cookies. May be frozen.

Applesauce Spice Cookies

Moist, hearty, and not too sweet, these cookies almost qualify as breakfast fare. They're also gluten free if made with GF oats, oat flour and baking powder.

2/3 cup (160 ml) unsweetened applesauce

1/2 cup (90 g) Sucanat (or other unrefined evaporated cane juice)

1/3 cup (80 ml) sunflower or other light-tasting oil, preferably organic

3 Tbsp (45 ml) finely ground flax seeds

1 tsp (5 ml) pure vanilla extract

1/2 tsp (2.5 ml) apple cider vinegar

1/3 cup (40 g) raisins

1 cup (90 g) quinoa flakes

1 cup (100 g) old-fashioned whole oats (not quick or instant) (see note)

1/2 cup (60 g) whole oat flour (see note)

1 tsp (5 ml) cinnamon

2 tsp (10 ml) baking powder (see note)

1/2 tsp (2.5 ml) baking soda

1/4 tsp (1 ml) fine sea salt

Preheat oven to 350F (180C). Line two cookie sheets with parchment paper, or spray with nonstick spray.

In a medium sized bowl, stir together the applesauce, Sucanat, oil, flax seeds, vanilla, vinegar and raisins. Set aside while you measure the dry ingredients, or at least 2 minutes.

In a large bowl, mix together the quinoa flakes, oats, oat flour, cinnamon, baking powder, baking soda and salt. Pour the wet mixture over the dry and stir to blend well.

Using a small ice cream scoop or tablespoon (15 ml), drop mounds of batter onto the cookie sheet about one inch (2.5 cm) apart. Wet your palms and press the cookies down to flatten until they are about 1/4 inch (6 mm) thick.

Bake in preheated oven for 25-28 minutes, rotating sheets about halfway through, until cookies are dry and browned on the edges. Allow to cool completely before removing from cookie sheets. Makes about 30 cookies. May be frozen.

> **Note:** For entirely gluten-free cookies, use GF brands of oats, oat flour and baking powder.

Banana Oat Bars

Partway between a cookie and a granola bar, this is my adaptation of an ancient recipe I had in my files. The original called for eggs, sugar, butter and wheat flour; this version is infinitely healthier, yet will charm you nonetheless. If you use certified GF oats, oat flour and baking powder, the recipe remains gluten-free. Top with a favorite frosting for a more decadent treat.

1/2 cup (90 g) Sucanat (or other unrefined evaporated cane juice)

1 Tbsp (15 ml) finely ground flax seeds

1/4 cup (60 ml) plain or vanilla soy or almond milk

1/4 cup (60 ml) sunflower or other light-tasting oil, preferably organic

1 tsp (5 ml) pure vanilla extract

2 medium, very ripe bananas (about 8 ounces or 225 g)

1/3 cup (40 g) raisins or dried cranberries (optional)

1-1/2 cups (160 g) old fashioned rolled oats (not instant) (see note)

1/2 cup (40 g) unsweetened shredded coconut

1/4 cup (30 g) whole oat flour (see note)

1/2 tsp (2.5 ml) baking powder (see note)

1/8 tsp (.5 ml) fine sea salt

Preheat oven to 350F (180C). Line an 8" (20 cm) square pan with parchment paper, or spray with nonstick spray.

In a medium bowl, combine the Sucanat, flax seeds, soymilk, oil and vanilla.

Cut the bananas into chunks and add to the bowl. Using a potato masher or large fork, mash the bananas into the mixture, leaving a few little chunks (about the size of peas) here and there. Stir in the raisins, if using. Set aside while you measure the dry ingredients, or at least two minutes.

In a large bowl, combine the remaining ingredients. Pour the wet mixture over the dry and stir well to combine. It may seem too wet for a bar dough; this is as it should be.

Scrape the mixture into the pan and smooth the top. Bake in preheated oven 40-45 minutes, rotating pan about halfway through, until the top is dry and a tester inserted in the center comes out clean. Cool in pan for 10 minutes, then turn out onto a rack to cool completely. Makes 12 bars. May be frozen.

> **Note:** For entirely gluten free Banana Oat Bars, ensure that you use GF brands of oats, oat flour and baking powder.

Butterscotch Blondies
with Chocolate Chips and Tart Cherries

CF NF SF

These are a favorite dessert in our house. They are rich-tasting, chewy, and the combination of rice syrup and maple syrup mimics a butterscotch flavor extremely well. I love the combination of cherries and chocolate, but you could stir in any additions you like as long as you keep the same proportions. One alternative that I enjoy is pistachios and dried cranberries, for instance.

1 cup (140 g) light spelt flour

3/4 cup (90 g) barley flour

1 tsp (5 ml) baking powder

1/2 tsp (2.5 ml) baking soda

1/4 tsp (1 ml) fine sea salt

1/3 cup (90 ml) brown rice syrup

1/3 cup (90 ml) pure maple syrup

1/3 cup (90 ml) sunflower or other light-tasting oil, preferably organic

1 Tbsp (30 ml) pure vanilla extract

1/4 tsp (1 ml) rum or butterscotch flavoring (optional)

1/2 cup (100 g) non-dairy chocolate chips

1/3 cup dried tart cherries (45 g) or cranberries (40 g)

Preheat oven to 350F (180C). Line an 8" (20 cm) square pan with parchment paper, or grease well and flour the pan (flouring is essential, as the blondies tend to stick to the bottom of the pan without the parchment).

In a medium bowl, sift together the spelt flour, barley flour, baking powder, baking soda and salt. Set aside.

In a large bowl, whisk together the brown rice syrup, maple syrup, oil, vanilla and flavoring (if using) until well blended. Gently stir in the chips and cherries.

Pour the dry mixture over the wet and stir to blend. You will have a fairly thick and sticky batter. Turn the batter into the prepared pan and smooth the top with a rubber spatula.

Bake in preheated oven for 20-25 minutes, rotating pan about halfway through, until a tester inserted in the center comes out just barely clean (a moist crumb or two is fine). Take care not to overbake, or these will dry out! The batter will fall a little as it cools; this is as it should be. Allow to cool completely in pan before cutting into squares. Makes 16 squares. May be frozen.

Carrot Raisin Oatmeal Cookies

A new and healthier twist on traditional oatmeal cookies. Chewy, not too sweet, and all-around yummy!

- **2-1/2 ounces (70 g) finely grated carrot (about 1/2 cup or 120 ml. firmly packed)**
- **1/2 cup (120 ml) sunflower or other light-tasting oil, preferably organic**
- **3/4 cup (180 ml) pure maple syrup**
- **1 tsp (5 ml) apple cider vinegar**
- **1 tsp (5 ml) pure vanilla extract**
- **1 Tbsp (15 ml) finely ground flax seeds**
- **3/4 cup (105 g) raisins**
- **1 cup (140 g) light spelt flour**
- **1 tsp (5 ml) baking powder**
- **1 tsp (5 ml) baking soda**
- **1/2 tsp (2.5 ml) Chinese 5 spice powder, or use 1/2 tsp (2.5 ml) ginger and 1 tsp (5 ml) cinnamon**
- **1 cup (100 g) old-fashioned rolled oats (not instant or quick cooking)**

Preheat oven to 350F (180C). Line 2 large cookie sheets with parchment paper, or spray with nonstick spray.

In a medium bowl, combine the carrots, oil, maple syrup, vinegar, vanilla and flax seeds, then stir in the raisins. Set aside while you measure the dry ingredients, or at least 2 minutes.

In a large bowl, sift the flour, baking powder, baking soda and Chinese 5 spice powder; stir briefly to mix. Add the oats and stir again to combine.

Pour the wet mixture over the dry and stir to blend well. Using a small ice cream scoop or tablespoon (15 ml), place mounds of the batter on the cookie sheet about an inch (2.5 cm) apart. Wet your palms (or use a silicon spatula) and flatten the cookies slightly.

Bake for 10-12 minutes, rotating sheets about halfway through, until cookies are golden on the edges and puffed in the middle. Allow to cool completely before removing from sheets (these will firm up as they cool). Makes about 30 cookies. May be frozen.

Cashew Chocolate Chip Cookies

These are a delicate cookie with a sandy, almost shortbread-like texture.

- **2/3 cup (160 ml) smooth natural cashew butter, at room temperature**
- **1 Tbsp (15 ml) coconut oil, preferably organic, melted**
- **1 Tbsp (15 ml) tahini (sesame paste)**
- **1/4 cup (60 ml) pure maple syrup**
- **1 tsp (5 ml) pure vanilla extract**
- **1/4 cup (25 g) finely ground flax seeds**
- **1/8 tsp (.5 ml) ground cardamom**
- **1/4 tsp (1 ml) baking soda**
- **1/4 tsp (1 ml) fine sea salt, if cashew butter is unsalted**
- **1/3 cup (70 g) dark chocolate chips (see note)**

Preheat oven to 350F (180C). Line a cookie sheet with parchment paper, or spray with nonstick spray.

In a medium bowl, blend the cashew butter, coconut oil and tahini until perfectly smooth. Add the maple syrup and vanilla and stir to mix well.

In a small bowl, stir the flax seeds with the cardamom, soda and salt. Sprinkle this mixture over the cashew butter mixture, and stir to blend well. Gently stir in the chocolate chips.

Using a small ice cream scoop or tablespoon (15 ml), scoop batter onto cookie sheet about 2 inches (5 cm) apart. Wet your palms (or use a silicon spatula) and flatten each cookie slightly.

Bake for 12-15 minutes, rotating sheet about halfway through, until golden on the edges. Allow the cookies to cool completely before removing from cookie sheet (they will firm up as they cool). Makes 8-10 cookies. May be frozen.

> **Note:** For entirely gluten-free cookies, ensure that you use GF chocolate chips.

Chocolate Chip Cookies

I used to love very dense, very chewy chocolate chip cookies. This is my version, using dates or date purée to reproduce some of that density as well as for added sweetness. Not quite as sweet as traditional versions, these are nevertheless immensely satisfying.

- **Heaping 3/4 cup (110 g) unsweetened dried dates (18-20 medium dates, not Medjool) (see note)**
- **2 Tbsp (30 ml) date soaking water (see note)**
- **1/2 cup (90 g) Sucanat (or other unrefined evaporated cane juice)**
- **1/4 cup (60 ml) pure maple syrup**
- **1 Tbsp (15 ml) finely ground flax seeds**
- **1 Tbsp (15 ml) pure vanilla extract**
- **1/2 tsp (2.5 ml) apple cider vinegar**
- **1/3 cup (80 ml) sunflower or other light-tasting oil, preferably organic**
- **2/3 cup (135 g) dairy-free chocolate chips**
- **1 cup plus 2 Tbsp (155 g) light spelt flour**
- **1/2 cup (60 g) barley flour**
- **2 Tbsp (30 ml) organic cornstarch**
- **1 tsp (5 ml) baking powder**
- **1/4 tsp (1 ml) baking soda**
- **1/4 tsp (1 ml) cinnamon (optional)**
- **1/4 tsp (1 ml) sea salt**

Preheat oven to 350F (180C). Line 2 cookie sheets with parchment paper, or spray with nonstick spray.

Place the dates in a heatproof bowl and add enough boiling water to cover them (poke down any dates that float up so that they are all submerged in water). Allow to stand for 5 minutes, then drain and reserve the soaking water (you'll need some of it for the cookies).

Place the drained dates, 2 Tbsp (30 ml) of the soaking water, Sucanat, maple syrup and flax seeds in a food processor and process until you have a very smooth paste (no large bits of date should be visible). Add the vanilla, vinegar and oil and process again to blend. Sprinkle with the chocolate chips and stir them in by hand, but do not process again. Set aside while you measure the dry ingredients, or at least 2 minutes.

In a large bowl, sift the spelt flour, barley flour, cornstarch, baking powder, baking soda, cinnamon and salt; stir briefly to mix. Pour the wet ingredients over the dry and stir to combine. You should have a soft and sticky dough that's just firm enough to hold its shape when scooped.

Using a small ice cream scoop or tablespoon (15 ml), drop mounds of dough about 2 inches (5 cm) apart on cookie sheets. Wet your hands and use your palms (or use a silicon spatula) to flatten the cookies slightly.

Bake in preheated oven for 10-15 minutes (less for moist and fudgy cookies, more for dry and crispy cookies), turning the sheets about halfway through, until the edges are golden and the cookies puff up. They will still be quite soft. Allow to cool completely before removing from the sheets (they will deflate and firm up as they cool). Makes about 2 dozen. May be frozen.

Note: If you have ready-made date purée (the only ingredients should be dates and water), you can use 1/2 cup or 135 g. of the purée in place of the dates and water.

Chocolate Mint Chocolate Chip Cookies

A popular vegan cookie company in Toronto sells a cookie similar to this, which I used to buy all the time. But at almost $6.00 for a pack of 10 small cookies, the price seemed too steep. I decided to try my hand at my own version, and came up with these delicacies. Even more appealing than the original, with a dense, chewy center, these are a hit with everyone who's ever tried them.

- **3-1/2 ounces (110 g) pitted dried unsweetened dates, chopped (about 25 dates, not Medjool) (see note)**
- **2 Tbsp of date soaking water (see note)**
- **1/2 cup (90 g) Sucanat (or other unrefined evaporated cane juice)**
- **1/3 cup (80 ml) pure maple syrup**
- **20-25 fresh mint leaves, chopped, or use 1/2 tsp (2.5 ml) pure mint extract**
- **2 tsp (10 ml) pure vanilla extract**
- **1 tsp (5 ml) apple cider vinegar**
- **1/3 cup (80 ml) sunflower or other light-tasting oil, preferably organic**
- **2/3 cup (135 g) dairy-free chocolate chips**
- **1-1/2 cups (210 g) light spelt flour**
- **1/4 cup (35 g) cocoa powder (preferably non Dutch process)**
- **1 tsp (5 ml) baking powder**
- **1 tsp (5 ml) baking soda**
- **1/4 tsp (1 ml) fine sea salt**

Preheat oven to 350F (180C). Line 2 cookie sheets with parchment paper, or spray with nonstick spray.

Place the dates in a heatproof bowl and pour enough boiling water over them to cover (poke down any dates that float up so that they are all submerged in water). Allow to stand for 5 minutes, then drain and reserve the soaking water (you'll need some of it for the cookies).

Place the drained dates, 2 Tbsp (30 ml) of the soaking water, Sucanat, maple syrup and fresh mint (or extract) in a food processor and process until you have a very smooth paste (be sure no large bits of date are visible). Add the vanilla, vinegar and oil and process again to blend. Sprinkle the chocolate chips over the mixture and stir them in by hand, but do not process again. Set aside while you measure the dry ingredients, or at least 2 minutes.

In a large bowl, sift the flour, cocoa, baking powder, baking soda and salt; stir briefly to mix. Pour the wet ingredients over the dry and stir to combine. You should have a soft and sticky dough.

Using a small ice cream scoop or tablespoon (15 ml), drop mounds of dough about 2 inches (5 cm) apart on cookie sheets. Wet your hands and use your palms (or use a silicon spatula) to flatten the cookies slightly.

Bake for 10-14 minutes, rotating sheets about halfway through, until the cookies puff up and the tops begin to crack. They will still be quite soft. Allow to cool completely before removing from the sheets (they will firm up as they cool). Makes about 2 dozen. May be frozen.

> **Note:** If you have ready-made date purée on hand (the only ingredients should be dates and water), you can use 1/2 cup (135 g) of the purée instead of the dates and boiling water.

Chocolate Peanut Butter Fudgies

These cookies present the ultimate mixture of chocolate and peanut butter, with a base that's crispy on the edges and chewy in the middle. No one will ever guess that they're housing some hidden eggplant in the batter! (If you're wary of the veggie in a cookie, don't fear—you can substitute unsweetened applesauce).

1/2 cup (120 ml) all-natural crunchy peanut butter, at room temperature

2/3 cup (120 g) Sucanat (or other unrefined evaporated cane juice)

1/4 cup (60 ml) sunflower or other light-tasting oil, preferably organic

1/2 cup (120 ml) pure maple syrup

1 Tbsp (15 ml) pure vanilla extract

1 tsp (5 ml) apple cider vinegar

1/3 cup (80 ml) cooked, puréed eggplant or unsweetened applesauce

1-1/2 cups (210 g) light spelt flour

1/3 cup (35 g) dark cocoa powder (preferably not Dutch process)

1 tsp (5 ml) baking powder

1 tsp (5 ml) baking soda

1/2 tsp (2.5 ml) fine sea salt

Preheat oven to 375F (190C). Line two cookie sheets with parchment paper, or spray with nonstick spray.

In a medium bowl, cream together the peanut butter, Sucanat and oil. Add the maple syrup, vanilla, vinegar and eggplant (or applesauce) and mix well.

In a large bowl, sift together the flour, cocoa, baking powder, baking soda and salt. Pour the wet mixture over the dry and stir to mix well. You should have a very soft and slightly sticky dough, but one that will hold its shape.

Using a small ice cream scoop or tablespoon (15 ml), drop mounds of dough onto the cookie sheets about 2 inches (5 cm) apart. Wet your palms (or use a silicon spatula) and flatten the cookies slightly, to about 1/4 inch or 6 mm thickness.

Bake in preheated oven for 10-13 minutes, rotating sheets about halfway through, until the cookies are puffed and cracked on top (they will still be quite soft). Cool completely before removing from the cookie sheets (they will firm up as they cool). Makes about 30 cookies. May be frozen.

Chocolate Shortbread Cookies

If you're a fan of shortbread, these buttery, sandy cookies will be sure to please. Not too sweet and very chocolatey, they also make the perfect tart crust for Chocolate Satin Tarts (page 142).

1/2 cup (120 ml) coconut oil, preferably organic, solid and at room temperature (see note)

1 cup plus 1 Tbsp (150 g) light spelt flour

1/4 cup (35 g) dark cocoa powder (preferably not Dutch process)

1/4 cup plus 2 Tbsp (60 g) Sucanat (or other unrefined evaporated cane juice)

1/4 tsp (1 ml) baking powder

1/8 tsp (.5 ml) fine sea salt

3 Tbsp (45 ml) pure maple syrup

Preheat oven to 350F (180C). Line a cookie sheet with parchment paper, or spray with nonstick spray.

In the bowl of a food processor, combine the coconut oil, flour, cocoa, Sucanat, baking powder and salt until evenly mixed and coconut oil has broken up completely. Add the maple syrup and whir again until you have a thick and relatively dry dough (it should stick together when pinched between your fingers).

Using a small ice cream scoop or tablespoon (15 ml), roll the dough into small balls and place about 1 inch (2.5 cm) apart on cookie sheets. Wet your palms (or use a silicon spatula), and flatten the cookies to about 1/4 inch (6mm) thickness.

Bake in preheated oven 12-15 minutes, rotating sheet about halfway through, until cookies are browned on the edges. Allow to cool 5 minutes before removing to a rack to cool completely. Makes 16-20 cookies. May be frozen.

> **Note**: If your room is warm enough that the coconut oil has melted, place it in the refrigerator until it solidifies again before using in this recipe.

Cinnamon Coffee Toffee Bars

These bars taste so decadent, it's hard to believe they are made with only 1/4 cup (60 ml) sunflower oil and no refined sugars. If you like the taste of cinnamon, you will adore these chewy, rich bars.

2 tsp (10 ml) instant coffee substitute or 1 tsp (5 ml) instant coffee

1 Tbsp (15 ml) water

1 Tbsp (15 ml) pure vanilla extract

1/2 cup (90 g) Sucanat (or other unrefined evaporated cane juice)

1/2 cup (120 ml) brown rice syrup

1/4 cup (60 ml) sunflower or other light-tasting oil, preferably organic

3/4 cup (85 g) toasted pecan halves or pieces

1 cup (140 g) light spelt flour

1/2 cup (60 g) barley flour

1 Tbsp (15 ml) (yes, 1 Tbsp!) cinnamon

1/2 tsp (2.5 ml) baking powder

1/8 tsp (1 ml) fine sea salt

Preheat oven to 350F (180C). Line a 9" (22.5 cm) square pan with parchment paper, or spray with nonstick spray.

In the bottom of a medium-sized bowl, dissolve the coffee substitute in the water and vanilla. Add the Sucanat and stir to dissolve somewhat. Mix in the brown rice syrup and oil, then stir in the pecan pieces to coat. Set aside.

In a large bowl, sift together the spelt flour, barley flour, cinnamon, baking powder and salt.

Add the wet mixture to the dry and mix well. Spread the batter evenly in the pan and smooth the top. Bake for 20-25 minutes, rotating pan about halfway through, until puffed on top and a tester inserted in center comes out clean but still moist (do not overbake!).

Allow bars to cool in pan (they will firm up as they cool). Once cool, cut into 9 large or 12 more reasonable bars. (If you can't wait for them to cool, they will still taste yummy, but the texture will seem a bit too soft.) May be frozen.

Classic Peanut Butter Cookies

This is my version of the childhood classic, with a crisp exterior and slightly sandy texture. You'll recognize the standard criss-cross pattern and intense peanut butter flavor.

- **3/4 cup (180 ml) all-natural, smooth or crunchy peanut butter (the only ingredient should be peanuts)**
- **1/3 cup (80 ml) maple syrup**
- **1/3 cup (80 ml) brown rice syrup**
- **1/4 cup (60 ml) sunflower or other light-tasting oil, preferably organic**
- **1 tsp (5 ml) pure vanilla extract**
- **2 Tbsp (15 g) finely ground flax seeds**
- **2 cups (280 g) light spelt flour**
- **1 tsp (5 ml) baking powder**
- **1/2 tsp (2.5 ml) baking soda**
- **1/2-1 tsp (2.5-5 ml) fine sea salt, to your taste (if the peanut butter is unsalted; otherwise, omit salt)**

Preheat oven to 375F (190C). Line 2 cookie sheets with parchment paper, or spray with nonstick spray.

In a medium bowl, whisk together the peanut butter, maple syrup, brown rice syrup, oil, vanilla and flax seeds (alternately, whir together in a food processor until smooth). Set aside while you measure the dry ingredients, or at least 2 minutes.

In a large bowl, sift the light spelt flour, baking powder, baking soda and salt. Pour the wet mixture over the dry and mix well (use your hands if necessary to blend all ingredients). You should have a fairy thick, but still pliable, dough that holds together.

Using about a tablespoon (15 ml) of dough per cookie, roll the dough into balls and place about 2 inches (5 cm) apart on cookie sheets. Using the tines of a fork, press down on the cookie once, then again to create a criss-cross pattern and to flatten the cookies.

Bake in preheated oven for 10-15 minutes, rotating sheets about halfway through, until cookies are deep golden brown on the edges and beginning to brown on top. Allow to cool completely before removing from cookie sheets. Makes about 2 dozen cookies. May be frozen.

Coconut Macaroons

One of the most requested cookies from Bake It Healthy, these sweet treats combine both ground almonds and coconut for an ultra chewy base. Tahini is a terrific source of calcium, yet the flavor isn't prominent here.

3/4 cup (135 g) natural raw almonds, with skin

2 Tbsp (15 g) finely ground flax seeds

1/8 tsp (.5 ml) fine sea salt

2 cups (135 g) shredded unsweetened coconut

1/4 cup (60 ml) pure maple syrup

1/4 cup (60 ml) light agave nectar

1/4 cup (60 ml) tahini (sesame paste)

1 tsp (5 ml) pure vanilla extract

1/2 tsp (2.5 ml) coconut extract (optional)

Preheat oven to 350F (180C). Line 2 cookie sheets with parchment paper, or spray with nonstick spray.

In the bowl of a food processor, whir the almonds, flax and salt together until they resemble a coarse meal, about the texture of cornmeal. The mixture should be very finely ground, without any identifiable pieces of almond visible. Add the coconut and pulse once or twice to combine.

Pour the maple syrup, agave nectar, tahini, vanilla and coconut extract over the dry ingredients. Process again until everything is incorporated and the mixture forms a sticky ball (you may need to stop and scrape down the sides of the processor bowl once or twice). Stop as soon as the mixture holds together to avoid grinding the coconut too fine.

Using a small ice cream scoop or tablespoon (15 ml), drop small mounds of the mixture onto the cookie sheets about 1 inch (2.5 cm) apart. Wet your palms (or use a silicon spatula) and flatten the cookies slightly.

Bake in preheated oven 10-12 minutes, rotating sheets about halfway through, until the cookies are deep golden brown on top. Cool completely before removing to a cooling rack (the cookies will firm up as they cool). Makes 14-16 cookies. May be frozen.

Dalmatian Cheesecake Brownies

This fantastic combination of a dark, not-too-sweet brownie topped with a layer of chocolate-dotted "cheesecake" makes a spectacular dessert for a special occasion. Don't tell people what's in the topping—they will never guess!

Cheesecake Topping:

1 pkg. (350 g. or 12 oz.) aseptically-packaged firm or extra-firm, silken tofu, such as Mori Nu (*not* the kind packed in a tub in water)

1/2 cup (120 ml) natural smooth cashew butter

1/2 cup (120 ml) light agave nectar

1 Tbsp (15 ml) freshly squeezed lemon juice

1 tsp (5 ml) pure vanilla extract

1/2 tsp (2.5 ml) pure almond extract

Pinch fine sea salt

2/3 cup (135 g) dairy-free chocolate chips

Brownie Base:

4 oz. (115 g) dried, pitted unsweetened dates (18-24 medium dates, not Medjool) (see note)

1/3 cup date soaking liquid (see note)

3/4 cup plus 2 Tbsp (155 g) Sucanat (or other unrefined evaporated cane juice)

1/4 cup (60 ml) pure maple syrup

1 Tbsp (15 ml) pure vanilla extract

2 Tbsp (30 ml) finely ground flax seeds

6 Tbsp (1/4 cup plus 2 Tbsp or 90 ml) sunflower or other light-tasting oil, preferably organic

1 cup (140 g) light spelt flour

6 Tbsp (1/4 cup plus 2 Tbsp or 45 g) whole oat flour

3/4 cup (90 g) dark cocoa powder (preferably not Dutch process)

1/4 tsp (1 ml) baking powder

1/2 tsp (2.5 ml) baking soda

1/4 tsp (1 ml) fine sea salt

Preheat oven to 350F (180C). Line a 9" (22.5 cm) square pan with parchment paper, or spray with nonstick spray.

Soak the dates for the brownie: In a small bowl, cover the dates with boiling water. Allow to soak while you make the cheesecake filling.

Prepare the cheesecake topping: In the bowl of a food processor, process the tofu and cashew butter until smooth and no pieces of tofu are visible. Add the agave nectar, lemon juice, vanilla, almond extract and salt and process again, stopping to scrape the sides of the bowl occasionally, until you have a perfectly smooth mixture. Turn the mixture into a medium-sized bowl, scraping as much as you can from the processor (use the tip on page 32), but don't bother to wash it (you'll use it again in a moment). Fold the chocolate chips into the cheesecake mixture. Set aside.

Make the brownie base: Drain the dates and reserve 1/3 cup (80 ml) soaking liquid. Using the same processor bowl, whir the dates and soaking liquid until they form a relatively smooth paste. Add the Sucanat and maple syrup and process again until smooth, allowing the Sucanat to dissolve as much as possible (don't worry if a few flecks of date are visible here and there). Add the vanilla, flax seeds and oil, and process to blend. Set aside while you measure the dry ingredients, or at least 2 minutes.

In a large bowl, sift together the spelt flour, oat flour, cocoa, baking powder, baking soda and salt. Pour the wet mixture from the processor over the dry ingredients and stir to mix well. Turn the batter into the prepared pan and smooth the top.

Bake the brownie layer in preheated oven for 15 minutes. Remove the partially baked brownie and pour the reserved cheesecake mixture over it, smoothing the top with a rubber spatula.

Bake for an additional 50-60 minutes, rotating pan about halfway through, until the top is deep golden brown and the cheesecake has begun to pull away from the sides of the pan (the regular testing methods don't work for this cake, as the center will test underdone even when the brownie is ready). The middle of the cake should jiggle just a little when you shake the pan, but the rest should be firm.

Allow to cool completely at room temperature, then cover and refrigerate. The brownie should be served cold. Makes 16-20 servings (it's very rich; a little goes a long way). May be frozen; defrost, covered, in the refrigerator overnight before serving.

> **Note:** If you have ready-made date purée (the only ingredients should be dates and water), you can use 1/2 cup or 135 g. of the purée in place of the dates and water.

Easiest Almond Cookies

I used to buy a similar cookie at the health food store, but could never resign myself to the exorbitant price. I decided to devise my own version of the treats—and ended up preferring these, which are softer and chewier than the original.

2 cups (12 ounces or 340 g) raw natural almonds, with skin (see note)
1/4 cup (25 g) finely ground flax seeds
1/2 tsp (2.5 ml) baking soda
1/4 tsp (1 ml) fine sea salt
1/4 cup (60 ml) agave nectar, light or dark
2 Tbsp (30 ml) sunflower or other light-tasting oil, preferably organic
1 tsp (5 ml) pure vanilla extract
1 tsp (5 ml) pure almond extract
1 Tbsp (15 ml) water, if necessary

Preheat oven to 350F (180C). Line two cookie sheets with parchment paper, or spray with nonstick spray.

In the bowl of a food processor, whir the almonds, flax, baking soda and salt until you have a very fine meal (it should be the consistency of a coarse cornmeal or fine breadcrumbs, with no large pieces of almond visible). Watch that you don't blend so long as to obtain almond butter, however!

Add the agave nectar, oil and extracts, and process again just until the mixture holds together and leaves the sides of the bowl. It should look like a moist dough. If mixture is too dry, add the water and pulse quickly to blend.

Using a small ice cream scoop or tablespoon (15 ml), scoop the dough and roll into balls; place them about 2 inches (5 cm) apart on the cookie sheets. Wet your palms (or use a silicon spatula) and press down to flatten each ball to about 1/4 inch (6 mm) thickness.

Bake in preheated oven for 8-10 minutes, rotating sheets about halfway through, until edges are barely golden brown and cookies are dry in the center (the tops will still be light). Allow to cool completely before removing from sheets, as the cookies firm up when cool. Makes 15-20 cookies. May be frozen.

> **Note:** Using already-toasted almonds in these cookies produces a dryer product. If you like, you can use blanched almonds, though you'll miss out on the extra fiber provided by the skins.

Fluffy Fruited Pancakes
page 43

Sweet Harvest Muffins
page 63

Sunshine Breakfast Loaf
page 62

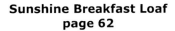

Glazed Almond Bars
page 89

Triple C Cookies
page 97

Dalmation Chesecake
Brownies
page 84

Classic Peanut Butter Cookies
page 82

Figaros
page 87

Seed Jumble Cookies
page 95

**Plum-Topped
Cornmeal Cake
page 124**

**Holiday Apple
Cake
page 119**

**Chocolate Layer Cake
with Fudgy Chocolate Frosting
page 108**

**Cinnmon Walnut
Coffee Cake
page 110**

**Mrs. K's Date Cake
page 122**

**Berries and Cream Tart
page 135**

Cocoa Nibbles
page 152

Fruity Cereal Chews
page 154

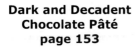

Dark and Decadent
Chocolate Pâté
page 153

Figaros

I really enjoy Fig Newtons, but I am just too lazy to roll out dough, fill it, and cut out the bars. I created this easy version of the classic bars during the winter, when grapefruits are abundant in the grocery stores. The tangy grapefruit makes a perfect foil for the sweet fig in the filling.

Filling:
1/2 cup (125 ml) freshly squeezed grapefruit juice

3 Tbsp (45 ml) agave nectar, light or dark

1 Tbsp (15 ml) freshly grated grapefruit zest

2 tsp (10 ml) freshly grated orange zest

10-1/4 ounces (290 g) soft dried figs (hard stems removed), cut in half

Cookie base and topping:
1/4 cup (60 ml) sunflower or other light-tasting oil, preferably organic

1/3 cup (80 ml) agave nectar, light or dark

1/2 tsp (2.5 ml) pure vanilla extract

2/3 cup (80 g) barley flour

1 cup (135 g) whole spelt flour

1/4 tsp (1 ml) baking powder

1/4 tsp (1 ml) baking soda

1/4 tsp (1 ml) fine sea salt

1/4 tsp (1 ml) cinnamon

1 Tbsp (15 ml) finely ground flax seeds

Preheat oven to 350F (180C). Line a 9" (22.5 cm) square pan with parchment paper, or spray with nonstick spray.

Make the filling: In a small, heavy-bottomed pot, combine the juice, 3 Tbsp (45 ml) agave nectar, grapefruit zest, orange zest and figs. Bring to a boil, then lower heat and simmer, covered, 5 minutes. Remove from heat and allow to cool for 10 more minutes.

Meanwhile, make the cookie base and topping: In a small bowl, whisk together the oil, 1/3 cup (80 ml) agave nectar and vanilla. Set aside.

In a large bowl, sift together the barley flour, spelt flour, baking powder, baking soda, salt and cinnamon. Add the flax and stir to combine.

Pour the wet mixture over the dry and stir until you have a soft dough. Pat about 2/3 of the dough into the bottom of the prepared pan (it will be a very thin layer). Spread the fig mixture evenly over the base, then crumble the rest of the cookie mixture over the top of the filling (there will not be enough dough left to cover all the filling; just crumble it in random bits and blobs, distributing it as evenly as possible).

Bake in preheated oven 25-30 minutes, rotating pan about halfway through, until edges are golden. Allow to cool completely before cutting into squares. Makes 12-16 squares. May be frozen.

> **Variation:** Use orange juice and 1 Tbsp plus 2 tsp (25 ml) orange zest in place of the grapefruit juice and zest.

Ginger Coconut Cookies

Redolent with ginger, these cookies are a chewy, spicy treat that's just decadent enough to bake as holiday gifts. But don't wait for the holidays—these are comforting all year round.

- **1/2 cup (120 ml) coconut oil, preferably organic, solid at room temperature (see note)**
- **1/2 cup (90 g) Sucanat (or other unrefined evaporated cane juice)**
- **1/4 cup (60 ml) blackstrap molasses**
- **1/3 cup (80 ml) pure maple syrup**
- **2 Tbsp (30 ml) finely ground flax seeds**
- **2 tsp (10 ml) freshly grated ginger root**
- **1 tsp (5 ml) pure vanilla extract**
- **2-1/4 cups (315 g) whole spelt flour**
- **1-1/2 tsp (7.5 ml) baking soda**
- **1/4 tsp (1 ml) fine sea salt**
- **1/2 tsp (2.5 ml) ground ginger**
- **2/3 cup (55 g) shredded unsweetened coconut**

Preheat oven to 350F (180C). Line 2 cookie sheets with parchment or spray with nonstick spray.

In the bowl of a food processor, whir together the coconut oil, Sucanat, molasses, maple syrup, flax seeds, fresh ginger and vanilla until smooth. Set aside while you measure the dry ingredients, or at least 2 minutes.

In a large bowl, sift together the flour, baking soda, salt and ground ginger. Add the coconut and stir to combine.

Pour the wet mixture over the dry and blend well, until you have a fairly stiff dough (you may need to use your hands to combine it fully). Using a small ice cream scoop or tablespoon (15 ml), measure mounds of dough and roll each into a ball. Place the balls of dough about 2 inches (5 cm) apart on cookie sheets and flatten slightly with the palm of your hand (or use a silicon spatula).

Bake for 10-13 minutes, rotating sheets about halfway through, until cookies are puffed, cracked slightly on top, and beginning to brown on the edges (they will still be soft to the touch). Allow to cool completely before removing from cookie sheets (they will firm up as they cool). Makes about 30 cookies. May be frozen.

> **Note:** If your room is warm enough that the coconut oil has melted, place it in the refrigerator until it solidifies before using in this recipe.

Glazed Almond Bars

Although the "glaze" on these bars is a bit unconventional (made with silken tofu), I was pleasantly surprised when they were a hit with virtually everyone who tried them, including my picky sister. The squares offer a buttery, rich base with a subtle almond flavor, topped with chopped almonds and a sticky, gooey glaze.

Glaze:

1/4 cup (60 ml) silken tofu, packed

2 Tbsp (30 ml) organic cornstarch

Pinch fine sea salt

1/4 cup (80 ml) light agave nectar

1/2 tsp (2.5 ml) pure almond extract

Base:

2 cups (280 g) light spelt flour

2-1/2 tsp (12.5 ml) baking powder

2 Tbsp (30 ml) finely ground flax seeds

1/4 tsp (1 ml) fine sea salt

1/2 cup (120 ml) packed coconut oil, preferably organic, solid at room temperature (see note)

2/3 cup (105 g) coarsely chopped natural almonds with skin (or use slivered almonds if you prefer)

2/3 cup (160 ml) light agave nectar

2 tsp (10 ml) pure vanilla extract

2 tsp (10 ml) pure almond extract

Preheat oven to 350F (180C). Line a 9" (22.5 cm) square pan with parchment paper, or spray with nonstick spray.

Make the glaze: In the bowl of a food processor, whir all ingredients until perfectly smooth and no traces of tofu are visible. Scrape into a small bowl and set aside.

Make the base: Using the same processor (no need to wash it), pulse together the flour, baking powder, flax seeds and salt. Drop the coconut oil by large tablespoons over the top, and process until well incorporated (the mixture should still look fairly dry and powdery). Pour the agave nectar, vanilla and almond extract over the flour mixture and process to a very soft, sticky dough.

Scrape the cookie base into the pan and spread evenly, smoothing the top. Sprinkle the almonds over the top as evenly as possible. Bake in preheated oven for 25 minutes, until the base begins to puff up and is light golden brown at the edges.

Remove from oven, drizzle with the glaze (it's all right if there are still some dry spots here and there; it will spread as it bakes), then rotate the pan and continue to bake for another 10-15 minutes, until the edges are browned and the glaze is mostly set (it might jiggle a bit in the middle; this is fine).

Cool completely before cutting into squares. Makes 9 large or 12 more reasonable bars. May be frozen.

> **Note:** If your room is warm enough that the coconut oil has melted, place it in the refrigerator until solid before using in this recipe.

Hazelnut Mocha Cookies

I found an intriguing recipe for these cookies in a magazine, but the original was filled with butter, caffeine, and lots of sugar. I decided to re-create the effect with a healthier array of ingredients, and came up with this winning combination.

- **1/2 cup (120 ml) brown rice syrup**
- **1/4 cup (60 ml) pure maple syrup**
- **2 Tbsp (30 ml) finely ground flax seeds**
- **4 Tbsp (60 ml) instant coffee substitute (yes, that much!)**
- **2 tsp (10 ml) pure vanilla extract**
- **1/2 tsp (2.5 ml) apple cider vinegar**
- **1/2 cup (120 ml) coconut oil, preferably organic, melted**
- **1/2 cup (75 g) lightly toasted hazelnuts, roughly chopped (I leave the skins on for more nutrients and fiber)**
- **1-1/2 cups plus 2 Tbsp (200 g) barley flour**
- **1-1/2 tsp (7.5 ml) baking powder**
- **1/2 tsp (2.5 ml) fine sea salt**

Preheat oven to 375F (190C) Line two cookie sheets with parchment paper, or spray with nonstick spray.

Pour the 1/2 cup (120 ml) brown rice syrup into a 2-cup (500 ml) glass measuring cup or bowl. Add the maple syrup for a total of 3/4 cup (180 ml) liquid. Stir in the flax seeds, coffee substitute, vanilla and vinegar, and mix well. Pour the melted coconut oil over all and stir to incorporate evenly (the mixture will thicken up a bit when you add the coconut oil). Gently stir in hazelnuts and set aside.

In a large bowl, sift the flour with the baking powder and salt. Pour the wet mixture over the dry and mix to create a soft dough.

Using a small ice cream scoop or tablespoon (15 ml), drop mounds of dough 2 inches (5 cm) apart onto cookie sheets (no need to flatten these, as they spread quite a bit while baking).

Bake in preheated oven for 12-14 minutes, rotating sheets about halfway through, until cookies are just turning golden on the edges and have puffed up a bit. Remove from oven and cool completely before removing from cookie sheets (they will firm up as they cool). Store in an airtight container. Makes about 24 cookies. May be frozen.

Macadamia Sesame Cookies

Light, crisp, with an intense sesame flavor and buttery texture, these simple yet delicious cookies will become a favorite in no time. Sesame seeds are high in calcium, adding to the nutritional value of these chewy, crunchy bites.

1/4 cup (80 g) natural smooth macadamia nut butter

2 Tbsp (30 g) tahini (sesame seed paste)

2 Tbsp (30 ml) sunflower or other light-tasting oil, preferably organic

1/3 cup (80 ml) pure maple syrup

1 tsp (10 ml) pure vanilla extract

1/4 tsp (1 ml) apple cider vinegar

1/2 cup (60 g) whole oat flour

1/4 cup plus 2 Tbsp (45 g) barley flour

1/2 tsp (2.5 ml) baking powder

1/2 tsp (2.5 ml) baking soda

1/4 tsp (1 ml) fine sea salt (if nut butter is unsalted; omit otherwise)

2 Tbsp (30 ml) raw sesame seeds

Preheat oven to 350F (180C). Line a cookie sheet with parchment paper, or spray with nonstick spray.

In a small bowl, whisk together the macadamia butter, tahini, oil, maple syrup, vanilla and vinegar. Set aside.

In a medium bowl, sift together the oat flour, barley flour, baking powder, baking soda and salt. Pour the wet mixture over the dry and stir well to combine.

Use a heaping teaspoon (5 ml) to drop the dough about an inch (2.5 cm) apart onto the cookie sheet. Wet your hands (or use a silicon spatula) and flatten the cookies until they are about 1/4 inch (6 mm) thick. Sprinkle each cookie with sesame seeds.

Bake in preheated oven for 12-15 minutes, rotating sheet about halfway through, until the cookies have cracked on top and the edges are golden. Allow to cool 5 minutes on the sheet before removing to a rack to cool completely. Makes 10-12 cookies. May be frozen.

Maple Walnut Cookies

Chewy with a crisp exterior, these cookies showcase the classic combination of walnuts and maple syrup. This recipe won a December, 2007 CookThink challenge for recipes with maple syrup.

1/2 cup (55 g) raw walnut halves or pieces
1/4 cup (30 g) finely ground flax seeds
1/4 cup plus 2 Tbsp (45 g) barley flour
1/4 tsp (1 ml) baking powder
1/4 tsp (1 ml) baking soda
1/4 tsp (1 ml) fine sea salt
2 Tbsp (30 ml) tahini (sesame paste)
1/3 cup (80 ml) pure maple syrup
1/2 tsp (2.5 ml) pure vanilla extract
1/4 tsp (1 ml) apple cider vinegar

Preheat oven to 350F (180C). Line two cookie sheets with parchment or spray with nonstick spray.

In the bowl of a food processor, process the walnuts, flax seeds, barley flour, baking powder, baking soda and salt until you have a fine meal the consistency of cornmeal (no large pieces of nut should be visible).

Add the tahini, maple syrup, vanilla and vinegar and pulse or process on low speed until the mixture comes together to form a sticky dough.

Using a small ice cream scoop or tablespoon (15 ml), scoop balls of dough and place on cookie sheets about 2 inches (5 cm) apart. Wet your palms (or use a silicon spatula) and flatten each cookie slightly.

Bake 8-12 minutes, rotating sheets about halfway through, until golden brown on the edges. Cool completely before removing from sheets (they will firm up as they cool). Makes about 15 cookies. May be frozen.

Pecan Coconut Chews—Raw or Baked!

When I first learned I could no longer eat wheat, I created these cookies, assuming "no wheat" meant "no flour of any kind." These days, I bake with alternate flours, but these cookies remain a grain-free favorite. Because the ingredients can all be eaten raw, you can also pat the mixture into a 9" (22.5 cm) square pan, refrigerate, and cut into squares for an equally delicious unbaked treat.

3-1/2 ounces or 110 g. (scant 1 cup) pitted dried unsweetened dates

Boiling water, to cover dates (see recipe instructions)

2 cups (235 g) raw pecan halves or pieces

Grated zest of one large orange

2 Tbsp (30 ml) Sucanat (or other unrefined evaporated cane juice)

1 Tbsp (15 ml) finely ground flax seeds

1/4 tsp (1 ml) ground ginger

1/8 tsp (.5 ml) fine sea salt

1 cup (80 g) shredded unsweetened coconut

1 tsp (5 ml) pure vanilla extract

Preheat oven to 350F (180C). Line two cookie sheets with parchment paper, or spray with nonstick spray.

Place the dates in a heatproof bowl and cover with boiling water. Allow to soak 5 minutes, then drain, reserving 1 Tbsp (15 ml) of the soaking water.

In the bowl of a food processor, whir together the pecans, orange zest, Sucanat, flax seeds, ginger and salt. Add the coconut and whir just to break the coconut up a bit.

Add the dates, the tablespoon (15 ml) date soaking water and vanilla, and process until the mixture comes together in a moist "dough."

Using a small ice cream scoop or tablespoon (15 ml), roll balls of dough and place on cookie sheets about an inch (2.5 cm) apart. Wet your palms (or use a silicon spatula) and flatten the cookies to about 1/4 inch (6 mm) thick. (Alternately, pat the mixture into a prepared 9" or 22.5 cm square pan and refrigerate for unbaked bars).

Bake for 12-15 minutes, rotating sheets about halfway through, until cookies are golden on the edges and dry on top. Allow to cool completely before removing from sheets. Makes about 20 cookies. May be frozen.

Pumpkinseed Shortbread Buttons

These rich-tasting cookies combine a subtle flavor with the typical sandy texture of conventional shortbread cookies made with butter.

1/2 cup (120 ml) smooth natural pumpkin seed butter, preferably organic at room temperature

1/4 cup (25 g) finely ground flax seeds

1/4 cup (60 ml) pure maple syrup

1 tsp (5 ml) pure vanilla extract

1/2 cup (75 g) brown rice flour

1/8 tsp (.5 ml) fine sea salt

Preheat oven to 350F (180C). Line a cookie sheet with parchment paper, or spray with nonstick spray.

In a medium bowl, whisk together the pumpkin seed butter, flax seeds, maple syrup and vanilla until creamy and evenly blended, or beat with electric beaters until combined. Add the flour and salt and mix well, until you have a fairly stiff dough.

Using a heaping teaspoon (5 ml), scoop the dough and roll into small balls, placing them about one inch (2.5 cm) apart on cookie sheet. Flatten slightly with your palm (or use a silicon spatula).

Bake for 10-12 minutes, rotating sheet about halfway through, until cookies are light golden brown. Allow cookies to cool completely before removing from the sheet.

Store in an airtight container in the refrigerator for up to 5 days. Makes 12 cookies. May be frozen.

Variation: For *Chocolate-Flecked Shortbread*, add about 1/4 cup (45 g) finely chopped dark chocolate to the batter along with the flour and salt; proceed as above. Alternately, you may use other nut or seed butters such as sunflower, sesame (tahini) or even almond butter in place of the pumpkin seed butter.

Seed Jumble Cookies

Reminiscent of a granola bar, these cookies are chock-full of seeds and flavor. And they're incredibly easy to make!

- **1/3 cup (80 ml) pure maple syrup**
- **1/3 cup (80 ml) agave nectar, light or dark**
- **2 tsp (10 ml) pure vanilla extract**
- **2 Tbsp (30 ml) natural smooth almond butter**
- **1/3 cup (80 ml) tahini (sesame seed paste)**
- **1-1/4 cups (130 g) old-fashioned whole rolled oats (not quick cooking or instant)**
- **1/4 cup (35 g) light spelt flour**
- **1/4 cup (35 g) finely ground flax seeds**
- **1/2 cup (70 g) sunflower seeds, raw or lightly toasted**
- **1/2 cup (75 g) pumpkin seeds, raw or lightly toasted**
- **1/2 cup (100 g) dairy-free chocolate chips**
- **1/3 cup (40 g) raisins or dried cranberries**
- **1/3 cup (50 g) sesame seeds, raw or lightly toasted**

Preheat oven to 350F (180C). Line 2 cookie sheets with parchment paper, or spray with nonstick spray.

In a small bowl, whisk together the maple syrup, agave nectar, vanilla, almond butter and tahini until smooth.

In a medium bowl, stir together the remaining ingredients. Pour the wet mixture over the dry and stir to combine well. The mixture will appear a bit crumbly and you may wonder if it will stick together enough; this is as it should be.

Using a small ice cream scoop or tablespoon (15 ml), drop mounds of the mixture about 2 inches (5 cm) apart on cookie sheets (you may need to press the edges a bit for it to hold together). Bake for 10-15 minutes, rotating sheets about halfway through, until golden. Allow to cool completely before removing from the sheets (cookies will firm up as they cool). Makes about 20 cookies. May be frozen.

Sugar-Free Sugar Cookies

These simple, not-too-sweet biscuits are the perfect base for cutouts or decorations. The dough remains soft and workable even when rolled and re-cut several times. These are great to make with the kids— and don't worry if they snack on the raw dough, as these don't contain eggs!

- **6 Tbsp (90 ml) light agave nectar**
- **1 Tbsp (15 ml) finely ground chia seeds**
- **2 Tbsp (30 ml) plain or vanilla soy or almond milk**
- **1 tsp (5 ml) pure vanilla extract**
- **1/2 tsp (2.5 ml) pure lemon extract**
- **2 cups (280 g) light spelt flour**
- **1-1/2 tsp (7.5 ml) baking powder**
- **1/4 tsp (1 ml) fine sea salt**
- **1/2 cup (120 ml) coconut oil, preferably organic, solid at room temperature (see note)**

Preheat oven to 350F (180C). Line two cookie sheets with parchment paper, or spray with nonstick spray.

In a glass measuring cup or small bowl, whisk together the agave nectar, chia seeds, soymilk, vanilla and lemon extract. Set aside while you prepare the other ingredients, or at least 2 minutes.

In a large bowl, sift together the flour, baking powder and salt. Whisk to combine evenly. Drop the coconut oil in large chunks over the flour mixture. Then, using your hands, pinch the mixture between your thumb and fingers repeatedly until it comes together and the oil is completely blended into the flour. The mixture should appear crumbly, but hold together when squeezed in your hand. (Note: the dough should *not* be the same as a pie dough, with visible, pea-sized bits of coconut oil distributed throughout; it should all be smoothly and completely blended into the flour.)

Pour the wet mixture over the dry and stir well to combine evenly. You should have a soft and slightly sticky dough, but one that holds together well.

To make drop cookies, use the dough immediately. Drop from a small ice cream scoop or tablespoon (15 ml) onto cookie sheets about 2 inches (5 cm) apart. Flatten slightly with your palm (or use a silicon spatula).

For rolled cookies, gather the dough together and form into a disk. Wrap the disk in plastic wrap and refrigerate until firm, about an hour. Once firm, remove the dough and roll out on a piece of waxed paper to about 1/4 inch (6 mm) thickness. Cut into desired shapes and place 2 inches (5 cm) apart on cookie sheets. Gather any remaining scraps of dough together and roll again; repeat until all the dough is used.

Bake the cookies in preheated oven for 10-13 minutes, rotating sheets about halfway through, until edges are golden. Cool completely before removing from the sheets and decorating as desired. Makes 24-30 cookies. May be frozen.

> **Note:** If your room is warm enough that the coconut oil has melted, place it in the refrigerator until it solidifies again before using in this recipe.

Triple C Cookies

Carob, Cashew and Cardamom—this unusual trio melds beautifully in this soft and chewy cookie with a subtle and mysterious spice. My husband was skeptical as he took a bite, then brightened and requested several more of these alluring treats!

1 tsp (5 ml) instant coffee substitute or 1/2 tsp (2.5 ml) instant coffee

1 tsp (5 ml) pure vanilla extract

1/2 cup (120 ml) pure maple syrup

1/4 cup (60 ml) brown rice syrup

1/4 cup (60 ml) sunflower or other light-tasting oil, preferably organic

1/2 cup (75 g) lightly toasted cashews, coarsely chopped

1-1/2 cups (200 g) whole spelt flour

2 Tbsp (30 ml) carob powder

1/4 tsp (2.5 ml) ground cardamom

1 tsp (5 ml) baking powder

1/2 tsp (2.5 ml) baking soda

1/4 tsp (1 ml) fine sea salt

Preheat oven to 350F (180C). Line 2 cookie sheets with parchment paper, or spray with nonstick spray.

In the bottom of a medium-sized bowl, dissolve the coffee substitute in the vanilla. Add the maple syrup, brown rice syrup and oil and whisk to blend well. Stir in the cashews to coat. Set aside.

In a large bowl, sift together the flour, carob powder, cardamom, baking powder, baking soda and salt. Pour the wet mixture over the dry and stir to blend well. You will have a very soft dough, but one that should more or less hold its shape.

Using a small ice cream scoop or tablespoon (15 ml), drop the dough onto prepared cookie sheets about 2 inches (5 cm) apart. Do not flatten the cookies.

Bake in preheated oven for 8-10 minutes, rotating sheets about halfway through, until edges are just beginning to brown and the cookies are a bit puffed and cracked on top. Allow to cool completely before removing from sheets (cookies will firm up as they cool). Makes 20-22 cookies. May be frozen.

Twice Spiced Ginger Biscuits

There's a brand of oatcakes available here that I love. When they came out with ginger-oat biscuits, I decided I had to try to make my own. These aren't quite like the original, but they have the crunchy, biscuit-like quality that I loved, with my own unique spice combination.

- **1/4 cup (60 ml) coconut oil, preferably organic, solid at room temperature (see note)**
- **1/4 cup (45 g) Sucanat (or other unrefined evaporated cane juice), plus more for tops**
- **1/4 cup (60 ml) pure maple syrup**
- **2 tsp (10 ml) freshly grated orange zest**
- **1/2 tsp (2.5 ml) pure vanilla extract**
- **1/2 tsp (2.5 ml) apple cider vinegar**
- **1-1/2 tsp (7.5 ml) finely ground flax seeds**
- **1 cup (140 g) light spelt flour**
- **1/3 cup (40 g) barley flour**
- **1/2 tsp (2.5 ml) baking powder**
- **1/2 tsp (2.5 ml) baking soda**
- **1/8 tsp (.5 ml) fine sea salt**
- **1/2 tsp (2.5 ml) Chinese 5 spice powder (or use cinnamon)**
- **1/2 tsp (2.5 ml) ground ginger**
- **1/4 cup (50 g) finely chopped candied ginger**

Preheat oven to 375F (190C). Line 2 cookie sheets with parchment paper, or spray with nonstick spray.

In the bowl of a food processor, blend the coconut oil and Sucanat until smooth. Add the maple syrup, orange zest, vanilla, vinegar and flax seeds and blend again. Set aside to allow the Sucanat to dissolve while you measure the dry ingredients.

In a large bowl, sift the spelt flour, barley flour, baking powder, baking soda, salt, 5 spice powder and ground ginger. Stir in the candied ginger and distribute well.

Process the wet ingredients once more to blend well. Pour the wet mixture over the dry, scraping the processor as clean as possible. Stir to combine, using your hands if necessary. You will have a fairly stiff dough.

Using a small ice cream scoop or tablespoon (15 ml), roll mounds of dough into balls and place about 2 inches (5 cm) apart on cookie sheets. Wet the bottom of a glass and then dip it in Sucanat; use the bottom to flatten each cookie to about 1/8 inch (3 mm) thickness, adding more Sucanat to the bottom of the glass as needed.

Bake in preheated oven 13-15 minutes, rotating sheets about halfway through, until golden on the edges and dry on top. Cool for 5 minutes on cookie sheets before removing to racks to cool completely. Makes 18-20 cookies. May be frozen.

> **Note:** If your room is so warm that the coconut oil has melted, place it in the refrigerator until it solidifies before using in this recipe.

Ultra Fudgy Brownies

One of the gripes of many vegan bakers is that it's too difficult to create brownies that are really fudgy instead of cakelike. Well, here they are: the ultimate fudgy brownies! The addition of puréed avocado creates a miracle of synergy with just 1/4 cup of oil, resulting in one of the richest-tasting, fudgiest brownies I've ever had.

- **1/4 cup (60 ml) packed puréed avocado flesh (about one small, ripe avocado)**
- **1 cup (180 g) Sucanat (or other unrefined evaporated cane juice)**
- **1/3 cup (80 ml) pure maple syrup**
- **1/4 cup (60 ml) sunflower or other light-tasting oil, preferably organic**
- **1 Tbsp (15 ml) finely ground flax seeds**
- **1/4 cup (60 ml) plain, vanilla or chocolate soy or almond milk**
- **2 tsp (10 ml) pure vanilla extract**
- **2 tsp (10 ml) instant coffee substitute or 1 tsp (5 ml) instant coffee**
- **1/3 cup (70 g) dairy-free chocolate chips**
- **3/4 cup (110 g) light spelt flour**
- **1/2 cup (60 g) barley flour**
- **3/4 cup (80 g) dark cocoa powder (preferably not Dutch process)**
- **1/2 tsp (2.5 ml) baking powder**
- **1/4 tsp (1 ml) baking soda**
- **1/2 tsp (2.5 ml) fine sea salt**

Preheat oven to 350F (180C). Line an 8" (20 cm) square pan with parchment paper or spray with nonstick spray.

In a medium bowl, combine the avocado purée and Sucanat; whisk to blend well. Add the maple syrup, oil, flax, soymilk, vanilla and coffee substitute and whisk well to dissolve the Sucanat and coffee substitute. Add the chocolate chips and stir gently just until they're coated in the wet mixture. Set aside while you measure the dry ingredients, or at least 2 minutes.

In a large bowl, sift together the spelt flour, barley flour, cocoa, baking powder, baking soda and salt. Pour the wet mixture over the dry and stir just to combine. The batter will be thick.

Turn the batter into the pan and spread evenly (you may need to hold down the corners of the parchment with your thumb as you spread the batter, or it might pull the paper with it as you spread it). Smooth the top.

Bake in preheated oven for 20-25 minutes, rotating pan about halfway through, until the edges look dry, the middle begins to rise, and a tester inserted in the center comes out just barely clean (it may still be moist). Do not overbake! (Longer baking time will result in cakelike brownies.)

Cool for at least 15 minutes, then refrigerate until completely chilled in order to slice into squares. The brownies will firm up while they chill. (Alternately, to remove the brownies from the pan, you can freeze the entire pan first, then turn the whole brownie out onto a cutting board or serving plate, peel away the parchment, and turn over onto a plate before cutting into squares.) Makes 9 large or 12 more reasonable squares. May be frozen.

Walnut Cinnamon Rounds

This is a staple recipe in my gluten-free cooking classes. Quick and easy, the cookies have a light taste and chewy texture that brings to mind Greek cuisine with their combination of lemon and cinnamon. And the walnuts provide some excellent Omega 3 fats to the mix!

2 cups (230 g) raw walnut halves

1/4 cup (30 g) finely ground flax seeds

Grated zest of one lemon

1/4 cup (35 g) brown rice flour

1-1/2 tsp (7.5 ml) cinnamon

1/2 tsp (2.5 ml) baking soda

1/4 tsp (1 ml) fine sea salt

1/4 cup (60 ml) agave nectar, light or dark

Preheat oven to 350F (180C). Line two cookie sheets with parchment paper, or spray with nonstick spray.

In the bowl of a food processor, whir the walnuts, flax seeds, lemon zest, rice flour, cinnamon, soda and salt until you have a very fine meal (there should be no chunks of walnut visible). Take care not to overmix, however, or you'll end up with nut butter!

Add the agave nectar and process again until the mixture begins to leave the sides of the processor bowl. It should look like a moist dough that holds together when squeezed between your fingers.

Using a small ice cream scoop or tablespoon (15 ml), roll mounds of dough into balls and place about 2 inches (5 cm) apart on cookie sheets. Wet your palms (or use a silicon spatula) and flatten each ball to about 1/4 inch (6 mm) thickness.

Bake in preheated oven for 8-10 minutes, rotating sheets about halfway through, until edges are golden and cookies are dry on top. Allow to cool completely before removing from sheets (these will firm up as they cool). Makes 15-20 cookies. May be frozen.

CAKES,

CUPCAKES

and TOPPINGS

Chocolate Layer Cake with Chocolate Buttercream Frosting

recipe, page 113

Tomato Spice Cake

recipe, page 127

Soy Free, Sugar Free Coconut Whipped Cream

recipe, page 125

Cakes, Cupcakes, Toppings and Frostings

Even though my parents rarely had money to spare and we kids lacked many of the material possessions enjoyed by my friends, in other ways, I'd say that my childhood was privileged. Every year on my birthday, for instance, I'd be presented with the most spectacular, elaborate birthday cake you could imagine, each a work of art designed specifically to reflect something about my age, the year, my current interests, or a key event in my life.

One year, there was a Barbie doll cake; on another occasion, a spotted chocolate-and-vanilla doggie confection; once, a cake shaped like the number "6" and later on, a tiered cake with pink flowers spilling onto the serving platter. But the one I remember best featured Little Bo Peep perched on a huge rectangular base, crook in hand and surrounded by her fluffy marshmallow sheep. My aunt, a caterer at the time, would design, bake and decorate each masterpiece for me and each of my sisters on our birthdays. Privileged, indeed.

When I started my organic baking business in 2005, I hadn't intended to make birthday cakes. But after literally dozens of requests, I relented. I labored to create a sugar-free buttercream frosting that would work well with my sugar-free cakes. Despite my less-than-stellar decorating skills, I was able to pipe basic flowers and birthday messages.

And then, the most magical thing occurred: calls began to pour in, as parents reported over and over how they'd never been able to find all-natural, sugar-free cakes or frostings before. More often than once, my basic little cake represented the first "real" birthday cake (complete with "Happy Birthday" message) a child--some of whom were eight or ten years old--had ever received *and* had also been able to eat. For me, that was, and still remains, the high point of owning my business.

Whether you're seeking layer cakes with sugar-free frosting for birthdays, bundt cakes for holiday tables, snack cakes for after-school munchies, or everyday cakes for dessert following a good meal, this chapter has some of what you're looking for.

Both the chocolate and vanilla cakes can be baked in layers, or you might opt instead for frosted cupcakes, with a few versions of sugar-free frosting (and some gluten-free as well). I love the rustic Plum-Topped Cornmeal Cake in late summer (sometimes even as a breakfast treat!), and the Cinnamon-Walnut Coffee Cake also makes a great addition to a brunch table. The Lemon Poppyseed Bundt Cake will impress guests when set out at a buffet. Or why not try out the quick and easy Mrs. K's Date Cake as a snack on a lazy weekend afternoon?

Whatever your dietary restrictions, you deserve to be privileged, too, with home-baked cake!

Blueberry Coffee Cake

My mom used to bake a wonderful blueberry coffee cake topped with a mix of cinnamon and sugar. Here's my revamped version, without the shortening, eggs, or white sugar: an easy, delicious cake that's really satisfying and not too sweet. It's perfect for a light dessert, yet also substantial enough to serve at brunch. Feel free to substitute other berries if you prefer.

Topping:
1/2 cup (55 g) chopped walnuts or pecans
1/4 cup (35 g) whole spelt flour
1/4 cup (30 g) whole rolled oats (not instant or quick-cooking)
2 tsp (10 ml) cinnamon
1 Tbsp (15 ml) sunflower or other light-tasting oil, preferably organic
1 Tbsp (15 ml) light agave nectar

Batter:
1/3 cup (80 ml) sunflower or other light-tasting oil, preferably organic
1/2 cup (120 ml) light agave nectar
1/2 cup (120 ml) plain or vanilla soy or almond milk
2 Tbsp (30 ml) finely ground flax seeds
Grated zest of one lemon
1 tsp (5 ml) pure vanilla extract
1 cup (135 g) whole spelt flour
3/4 cup (105 g) light spelt flour
1 Tbsp (15 ml) baking powder
1/4 tsp (1 ml) fine sea salt
2 cups (480 ml) blueberries, fresh or frozen (do not thaw if frozen)

Preheat oven to 350F (180C). Line a 9" (22.5 cm) square baking pan with parchment paper, or spray with nonstick spray.

Prepare the topping: in a small bowl, blend the nuts, 1/4 cup whole spelt flour, oats and cinnamon. In another small bowl, mix together the 1 Tbsp (15 ml) oil and 1 Tbsp (15 ml) agave nectar. Pour the agave mixture over the dry ingredients and toss until crumbly. Set aside.

Mix the batter: in a medium bowl, combine the 1/3 cup (80 ml) oil, 1/2 cup (120 ml) agave nectar, soymilk, flax seeds, lemon zest and vanilla. Set aside while you prepare the dry ingredients, or at least 2 minutes.

In a large bowl, sift together the 1 cup (135 g) whole spelt flour, light spelt flour, baking powder and salt. Pour the wet ingredients over the dry and stir just to blend (it's okay if a few small dry spots remain here or there). Gently fold one cup (240 ml) of the blueberries into the batter. Spread batter in pan.

Sprinkle the top of the cake first with the topping mixture, then sprinkle the remaining blueberries over all.

Bake for 45-50 minutes, rotating pan about halfway through, until a cake tester inserted in the center comes out clean. Serve warm or at room temperature. Makes 9 large or 16 small squares. May be frozen.

Carrot Snack Cake

Moist and delicious yet not too sweet, this is a perfect after school snack.

- **1-1/2 cups (155 g) finely grated carrot, unpacked (about 2 large carrots)**
- **1 Tbsp (10 ml) finely ground flax seeds**
- **1/2 cup (120 ml) agave nectar, light or dark**
- **3/4 cup (180 ml) plain or vanilla soy or almond milk**
- **1/3 cup (80 ml) sunflower or other light-tasting oil, preferably organic**
- **1 tsp (5 ml) pure vanilla extract**
- **1/2 tsp (2.5 ml) apple cider vinegar**
- **1/2 cup (70 g) raisins**
- **1 Tbsp (15 ml) freshly grated lemon zest, or 1/2 tsp (2.5 ml) lemon extract**
- **1-1/2 cups (205 g) whole spelt flour**
- **2 tsp (10 ml) cinnamon**
- **1/2 tsp (2. 5 ml) ground ginger**
- **2 tsp (10 ml) baking powder**
- **1/2 tsp (2.5 ml) baking soda**
- **1/4 tsp (1 ml) fine sea salt**
- **1/2 cup (40 g) unsweetened shredded coconut**

Preheat oven to 350F (180C). Line a 9" (22.5 cm) square pan with parchment paper, or spray with nonstick spray.

In a medium bowl, combine the carrots, flax seeds, agave nectar, soy milk, oil, vanilla, vinegar, raisins and lemon zest. Set aside while you measure the dry ingredients, or at least 2 minutes.

In a large bowl, sift together the flour, cinnamon, ginger, baking powder, baking soda and salt. Stir briefly to distribute the spices. Add the coconut and stir to combine.

Pour the wet ingredients over the dry and stir just to combine (it's okay if a few dry spots remain here and there). Pour the batter into the prepared pan and smooth the top.

Bake in preheated oven for 25-35 minutes, rotating pan about halfway through, until a tester inserted in the center comes out clean. Cool in pan. Makes 12-16 servings. May be frozen.

Cashew "Cream"

A staple in most vegan households, cashew cream is a versatile topping that can be used instead of ice cream or whipped cream atop fruit desserts, pies, or hot cereals. My version is also made without any added sugar and with "live" ingredients. Soaking the nuts results in a smoother, creamier "cream."

1 cup (150 g) raw cashews, soaked in room-temperature water for 4-6 hours

10-14 pitted dried dates, soaked in room-temperature water for 4-6 hours

1 tsp (5 ml) pure vanilla extract

3/4-1 cup (180-240 ml) plain or vanilla soy or almond milk (or use a combination of milk and the date soaking water)

Drain the cashews and dates (reserve the date soaking water, if desired, to use instead of soymilk) and place in a blender. Add the remaining ingredients and blend (in batches, if necessary) until very smooth and creamy (about 10 minutes). Add liquid as needed, and push mixture down toward center blades frequently.

Once it is smooth, continue to blend for another minute until the mixture is perfectly creamy and velvety. Refrigerate until ready to serve. Makes about 2 cups (480 ml).

Chocolate Ganache Frosting

The trademark richness and velvety texture of conventional ganache is normally derived from dairy cream. In this recipe, avocado reproduces the glossy richness to spectacular result, completely cholesterol-free. Use this as an indulgent filling or topping for your favorite cake or cupcakes.

4 ounces (115 g) dairy-free semisweet chocolate, chopped, or chocolate chips

2 Tbsp (30 ml) plain or vanilla soy or almond milk

1/4 cup (60 ml) packed avocado purée (from a barely-ripe avocado; a very ripe avocado is not suitable here), about 1/2 medium avocado

1/4 cup (60 ml) pure maple syrup

2 tsp (10 ml) pure vanilla extract

3 Tbsp (30 g) cocoa powder (preferably not Dutch process)

Pinch fine sea salt

In a large heatproof bowl set over a small pan of simmering water (the bottom of the bowl should sit above the water without touching it), melt the chocolate and soymilk; stir to blend well. Set aside.

In the bowl of a food processor, whir the avocado, maple syrup, vanilla, cocoa and salt. Add the still-warm chocolate mixture, and whir to blend well, scraping down sides of processor bowl as needed. The mixture should be glossy and dark, with a pudding-like consistency.

Turn the ganache into a bowl, cover, and refrigerate until cold, at least 3 hours. Once chilled, it should thicken and become spreadable. If the ganache is too thick, return it to the processor and blend again until smooth and spreadable. Makes about 1 cup, enough to frost a single layer or 8-10 cupcakes. Recipe may be doubled. May be frozen (defrost in a covered container overnight in the refrigerator, then re-blend before using).

Chocolate Layer Cake

There are many versions of a vegan chocolate cake in cookbooks and on the Internet. After experimenting with almost all of them, I came up with this version of my own. The addition of orange juice adds a depth of flavor without a discernible orange taste, and the resulting cake is incredibly light. This cake received raves from virtually all the customers for whom I baked it for birthdays and special occasions.

- **4 tsp (1 Tbsp plus 1 tsp or 20 ml) instant coffee substitute, or 1-1/2 tsp (7.5 ml) instant coffee**
- **1 Tbsp (15 ml) pure vanilla extract**
- **2/3 cup plus 3 Tbsp (150 g) Sucanat (or other unrefined evaporated cane juice)**
- **3 level Tbsp (15 g) finely ground flax seeds**
- **1/2 cup (120 ml) pure orange juice**
- **3/4 cup (180 ml) water**
- **2 Tbsp (30 ml) apple cider vinegar**
- **1-3/4 cups (245 g) light spelt flour**
- **1/4 cup plus 3 Tbsp (50 g) dark cocoa powder (preferably not Dutch process)**
- **1 tsp (5 ml) baking powder**
- **3/4 tsp (3.5 ml) baking soda**
- **1/2 tsp (2.5 ml) fine sea salt**

Preheat oven to 350F (180C). Line two 8" (20 cm) round pans with parchment paper, or spray with nonstick spray.

In the bottom of a medium bowl, dissolve the instant coffee substitute in the vanilla. Add the Sucanat, flax seeds, orange juice, water and vinegar, and whisk to dissolve the Sucanat somewhat. Set aside while you measure the dry ingredients, or at least 2 minutes.

In a large bowl, sift together the flour, cocoa, baking powder, baking soda and salt. Add the wet ingredients to the dry and whisk just to blend (the mixture will begin to bubble a bit; do not overmix!).

Divide the batter evenly between the two pans (you can weigh it, or just estimate by setting the pans side by side on a counter as you pour and aiming for equal levels). Smooth the tops.

Bake in preheated over for 35-40 minutes, rotating the pans about halfway through, until a tester inserted in the center of each pan comes out clean (depending on where they were situated in the oven, the two layers may not be ready at exactly the same time). Cool in pan at least 15 minutes before cutting.

If you will be frosting the cake, this works best if you freeze the cake for an hour or two first, then remove from the pan and frost while still frozen, as this helps prevent crumbling (the cake is quite delicate otherwise). Frost as desired. Makes 8-10 servings. May be frozen (depending on frosting used).

Chocolate Mystery Cupcakes

When I first started creating alternative baked goods, my zeal to include vegetables in every item led me to this recipe, originally a chocolate lava cake. To my delight, the cakes won a blog contest for favorite vegetable-based recipe! I've since decided I prefer these as cupcakes with chocolate chips scattered throughout, as it's important to cool the cakes to eliminate any trace of spinach flavor (promise!)

> **2 ounces (70 g) fresh or frozen spinach (you may include the stems)**
> **3-1/2 ounces (100 g) grated zucchini, fresh or frozen (about 1 cup, unpacked)**
> **1/4 cup (60 ml) plain or vanilla soy or almond milk**
> **1/3 cup (80 ml) agave nectar, light or dark**
> **1/8 cup (30 ml) pure maple syrup**
> **1/4 cup (60 ml) sunflower or other light-tasting oil, preferably organic**
> **1 Tbsp (15 ml) finely ground flax seeds**
> **1/2 tsp (2.5 ml) apple cider vinegar**
> **2 tsp (10 ml) pure vanilla extract**
> **2 tsp (10 ml) instant coffee substitute, or 1 tsp (5 ml) instant coffee**
> **1 cup (140 g) light spelt flour**
> **1/2 cup (60 g) whole oat flour**
> **1/3 cup (40 g) dark cocoa powder (preferably not Dutch process)**
> **1-1/2 tsp (7.5 ml) baking powder**
> **3/4 tsp (3.5 ml) baking soda**
> **1/4 tsp (1 ml) fine sea salt**
> **2/3 cup (270 g) dairy-free chocolate chips**

Preheat oven to 350F (180C). Line 12 muffin cups with paper liners, or spray with nonstick spray (or spray 24 mini muffin cups).

In a food processor or blender, blend the spinach and zucchini to a paste. Add the soymilk, agave nectar, maple syrup, oil, flax seeds, vinegar, vanilla and coffee substitute and process again until smooth. (There may be a few small flecks of spinach visible; this is fine).

In a large bowl, sift together the spelt flour, oat flour, cocoa, baking powder, baking soda and salt. Pour the wet mixture over the dry and top with the chips. Stir well to combine.

Using a large ice cream scoop or 1/3 cup (80 ml) measuring cup, fill the muffin cups about 3/4 full. Bake in preheated oven 35-40 minutes, rotating pan about halfway through, until a tester inserted in a center cupcake comes out clean. Allow to cool 5 minutes before removing to a cooling rack. *Cool completely before sampling*—the flavor changes as they cool, and any trace of veggies disappears in the cold cupcakes. Frost if desired. May be frozen.

Cinnamon Walnut Coffee Cake

One of the first recipes I created for my company, Bake It Healthy, was this cake. A lighter, cholesterol-free version of a dense coffee cake of my youth, this is nonetheless still a special treat, filled and topped with a rich cinnamon-walnut crumble.

Topping/Filling:

1/4 cup (30 g) old-fashioned whole rolled oats (not instant or quick-cooking)

1/3 cup (60 g) Sucanat (or other unrefined evaporated cane juice)

1/2 cup (70 g) whole spelt flour

1/2 cup (55 g) walnut pieces or coarsely chopped walnuts

1 Tbsp (15 ml) cinnamon

2 Tbsp (30 ml) sunflower or other light-tasting oil, preferably organic

Cake:

3-1/2 ounces (110 g) pitted dried unsweetened dates, chopped (about 25 dates, not Medjool) (see note)

1/3 cup (80 ml) boiling water (see note)

1/2 cup (120 ml) plain or vanilla soy or almond milk

1/2 cup (120 ml) pure maple syrup

1/3 cup (80 ml) sunflower or other light-tasting oil, preferably organic

1 heaping Tbsp (15 ml) finely ground flax seeds

1 Tbsp (15 ml) pure vanilla extract

3/4 cup (110 g) light spelt flour

3/4 cup (105 g) whole spelt flour

1-1/2 tsp (7.5 ml) baking powder

1/2 tsp (2.5 ml) baking soda

1/4 tsp (1 ml) fine sea salt

Preheat oven to 350F (180C). Line the bottom of an 8" (20 cm) round pan with parchment, or spray with nonstick spray.

Make the topping/filling: In a medium bowl, combine the oats, Sucanat, 1/2 cup whole spelt flour, walnut pieces and cinnamon. Drizzle with the 2 Tbsp (30 ml) oil and toss with your hands until the mixture is evenly moistened and crumbly. Set aside.

Make the cake: In a small heatproof bowl or measuring cup, pour the boiling water over the dates; cover and allow to sit for 5 minutes. Place both the dates and soaking water into the bowl of a food processor and process briefly until almost smooth. Add the soymilk, maple syrup, 1/3 cup (80 ml) oil, flax seeds and vanilla, and process again until well combined; ensure that there are no large lumps of date visible. Set aside while you measure the dry ingredients, or at least 2 minutes.

In a large bowl, sift together the light spelt flour, 3/4 cup (105 g) whole spelt flour, baking powder, baking soda and salt. Pour the wet ingredients over the dry and stir to blend; don't worry if there are a few little dry spots here or there.

Spread about half the plain batter into the pan (you can just estimate). Sprinkle with about 1/2 of the topping, then, using a spoon, dot the rest of the batter over the top, covering as much of the topping as you can. Use the back of a spoon to spread the top layer of batter over any empty spaces, covering as much of the filling as you can with batter.

Sprinkle with the remainder of the filling, covering the batter as best you can (it's okay if a few empty spots are left here and there). Press the topping lightly into the top of the cake.

Bake in preheated oven for 55 to 60 minutes, rotating pan about halfway through, until a tester inserted in the center comes out clean but moist. The cake should also feel firm when pressed lightly with your finger.

Cool completely in pan before removing to a serving plate (it helps to refrigerate the cake first before removing it). Store wrapped in plastic or in a covered container in the refrigerator. Makes 8 servings. May be frozen.

> **Note:** If you have ready-made date purée on hand (the only ingredients should be dates and water), you can use 1/2 cup or 135 g. of the purée in place of the dates and water.

Coconut Mini-Loaves or Cupcakes

These cakes are light and not too sweet, with a pronounced coconut flavor. For fancier loaves, drizzle with your favorite glaze, or bake as cupcakes and frost as desired.

2 Tbsp (30 ml) coconut oil, preferably organic, melted

2 Tbsp (30 ml) smooth natural cashew or macadamia nut butter, at room temperature

2/3 cup (180 ml) light agave nectar

1 Tbsp (15 ml) pure vanilla extract

1/3 cup (80 ml) plain or vanilla soy, almond or rice milk

1/4 tsp (1 ml) pure coconut extract (optional)

1 Tbsp (15 ml) finely ground flax seeds

1/4 cup (30 g) garbanzo bean (chickpea) flour

1/4 cup (40 g) whole bean flour

1/4 cup (30 g) sorghum flour

1/4 cup (45 g) potato starch

1-1/4 tsp (6 ml) baking powder (see note)

1/4 tsp (1 ml) baking soda

1/4 tsp (1 ml) xanthan gum

1/4 tsp (1 ml) fine sea salt

1/2 cup (40 g) shredded unsweetened coconut

Preheat oven to 350F (180C). Line 6 mini loaf pans or 9 muffin cups with paper liners, or spray with nonstick spray. If using individual loaf pans, place them on a cookie sheet.

In a medium bowl, whisk together the coconut oil and cashew butter. Slowly stir in the agave nectar, vanilla, soymilk, coconut extract and flax seeds; whisk to combine. Set aside while you measure the dry ingredients, or at least 2 minutes.

In a larger bowl, sift together the garbanzo flour, whole bean flour, sorghum flour, potato starch, baking powder, baking soda, xanthan gum and salt. Whisk to combine. Add the coconut and stir to blend.

Pour the wet ingredients over the dry and stir to mix well. Using a large ice cream scoop or 1/3 cup (80 ml) measuring cup, fill the loaf pans or cupcake cups about 3/4 full.

Bake in preheated oven for 25-30 minutes, rotating the cookie sheet about halfway through, until a tester inserted in a center loaf comes out clean (the tops will begin to crack and brown a bit). Cool in pans for 5 minutes before removing to a rack to cool completely. Makes 6 mini-loaves or 9 cupcakes. May be frozen.

Note: for entirely gluten-free loaves, ensure that you use a GF brand of baking powder.

Fudgy Chocolate Frosting or Buttercream

This is my "go-to" frosting when I need something that's reliable and easy to use. It spreads, it pipes, it holds up at room temperature. . . and it's both sugar-free <u>and</u> chocolate flavored! A great all-purpose frosting.

6 Tbsp (80 g) refined coconut oil, preferably organic (see note 1)

3 Tbsp (20 g) organic cornstarch

3 Tbsp (20 g) dark cocoa powder (preferably not Dutch process)

Pinch fine sea salt

1/3 cup (80 ml) light agave nectar

6 Tbsp (50 g) light spelt flour

3/4 cup (180 ml) plain, vanilla or chocolate soy or almond milk

1 tsp (5 ml) pure vanilla extract

In the bowl of a food processor, combine the coconut oil, cornstarch, cocoa and salt, and blend to a paste. Be sure to scrape the sides and bottom of the bowl, lifting the blades to scrape under them, to ensure that all the starch and cocoa are incorporated. Set aside.

In a small, heavy-bottomed pot, whisk together the agave nectar and flour until very smooth and no lumps are visible. Slowly add the soymilk until blended. (Blending the agave with the flour first helps to eliminate any lumps that might form when the frosting is cooked).

Now, get ready for some muscle power! Using a silicon spatula or whisk, cook the mixture over medium heat, stirring constantly, until it begins to thicken; it will thicken on the bottom of the pot fairly quickly, and you'll need to stir vigorously to prevent clumps from forming. Reduce heat to medium-low and continue to cook and stir for one minute, scraping the bottom with the whisk or spatula to ensure it doesn't scorch, until the mixture is uniformly thick and attains the texture of a very thick paste. Remove from heat and stir in the vanilla (it should be too thick to use as frosting at this point).

Add the hot agave mixture to the processor bowl and blend again, scraping sides if necessary, until everything comes together in a thick, glossy spread (if it refuses to come together and the oil separates out, add more soymilk, *one teaspoon at a time*, and blend again until it reaches this texture. Resist the temptation to add more milk at one time; this frosting can transform from being too thick to being too thin really quickly.) It will be dark, shiny, and look almost like a cooked pudding, but still be thick enough to hold its shape.

To use as a fudgy frosting, cover the surface with plastic wrap (to prevent a skin from forming) and allow the mixture to cool to room temperature. Stir and then spread on a cake or cupcakes.

For a lighter frosting with a buttercream texture, pour the mixture into a deep bowl, cover with plastic wrap and refrigerate until very cold (at least an hour).

Once cold, beat the frosting with electric beaters at high speed, scraping sides of bowl frequently, until it turns a shade or two lighter, thickens and becomes fluffy (2-3 minutes). When you first start to beat it, it will remain thick and glossy, and you may wonder if it will transform into a spreadable frosting; but keep beating, and it will soften and lighten up, eventually becoming fluffy (see note 2). Once beaten, spread the frosting on a cake or cupcakes, or pipe as desired.

Makes enough to frost a small layer cake, large rectangular cake, or 12 cupcakes. Store in refrigerator, but bring to room temperature before serving. May be frozen (defrost overnight in a covered container in the refrigerator, then beat again before using).

Note 1: You can certainly use unrefined coconut oil in this recipe, but there will be a pronounced coconut flavor.

Note 2: The final thickness of the frosting will depend on the exact heat of your stove, the pot you used, and the exact time that the frosting was cooked. Because of these slight variations, your final frosting may turn out slightly thicker or slightly thinner than mine.

If you find it is too thick to spread even after it's beaten, try this: add a bit more milk, *one teaspoon at a time*, and beat again until you reach the desired consistency. (Resist the temptation to add more milk at one time; this frosting can transform from being too thick to being too thin really quickly).

If you find it is too thin to spread and is almost pudding-like, try this: return the frosting to the refrigerator until it is very cold. Melt an additional 2 Tbsp (30 ml) coconut oil in a small bowl, and then pour over the cold frosting; beat again to incorporate the coconut oil. The frosting should thicken up nicely and become fluffy.

Glazed Lemon Poppyseed Bundt Cake

A big, light lemon cake dotted with a generous helping of poppyseeds and a tart lemon glaze. This cake will serve a crowd and is sure to impress.

Cake:

Freshly grated zest of 3 very large or 4 small lemons

1/4 cup (40 g) Sucanat (or other unrefined evaporated cane juice)

1/3 cup (80 ml) freshly squeezed lemon juice, plus enough water to make 3/4 cup (180 ml) liquid

3 Tbsp (45 ml) finely ground flax seeds

3/4 cup (180 ml) plain or vanilla soy or almond milk

2/3 cup (160 ml) sunflower or other light-tasting oil, preferably organic

2 tsp (10 ml) pure vanilla extract

2 tsp (10 ml) pure lemon extract

1 tsp (5 ml) apple cider vinegar

2 Tbsp (30 ml) poppyseeds

3-3/4 cups (535 g) light spelt flour

1-1/2 tsp (7.5 ml) baking powder

2 tsp (10 ml) baking soda

1 tsp (5 ml) fine sea salt

Glaze:

Freshly squeezed juice of one lemon plus enough water to equal 2/3 cup liquid (160 ml)

1/4 cup (60 ml) light agave nectar

Make the cake: Preheat oven to 350F (180C). Lightly grease a large bundt pan with coconut oil, or spray with nonstick spray.

In a large bowl, combine the lemon zest, Sucanat and lemon juice-water mixture. Stir to dissolve the Sucanat somewhat. Add the flax seeds, soymilk, oil, vanilla, lemon extract, vinegar and poppyseeds, and whisk to blend. Set aside while you measure the dry ingredients, or at least 2 minutes.

In a large bowl, sift together the flour, baking powder, baking soda and salt. Pour the wet ingredients over the dry, and, using a whisk, stir quickly just to combine (the mixture may begin to foam and bubble a bit; this is as it should be). Do not overmix! Immediately turn the batter into the prepared pan and smooth the top as best you can.

Bake in preheated oven for 55 minutes to one hour, rotating pan about halfway through, until a tester inserted halfway between the outside and inside walls of the pan comes out clean. Allow to cool 10 minutes in the pan before turning out onto a rack to cool completely. Spoon the glaze over the top, allowing it to soak into the cake and drip down the sides. Garnish with more lemon zest, if desired. Makes 20-24 servings. May be frozen.

While the cake bakes, make the glaze: In a small, heavy-bottomed pot, combine the lemon juice-water mixture and agave nectar. Bring to a boil over medium heat, then lower heat to medium-low and allow to bubble, stirring occasionally, until the mixture thickens, darkens in color and is reduced to about 1/4 cup (60 ml) . Allow to cool 5 minutes before glazing the cake.

Gluten Free, Sugar Free, Soy Free
Chocolate "Buttercream" Frosting

Since regular frostings rely on sugar for most of their substance, it can be a challenge to make gluten-free frosting without any sugar at all. This one requires a few steps, but it's worth it: the result is a very versatile frosting that can be spread or piped. It also retains its shape at room temperature.

- **1/4 cup (40 g) potato starch**
- **1/4 cup (35 g) dark cocoa powder (preferably not Dutch process)**
- **1/3 cup (80 g) refined coconut oil, preferably organic (see note)**
- **1/2 cup (80 g) organic cornstarch, divided**
- **1/2 cup (120 ml) agave nectar, light or dark**
- **1/2 cup (120 ml) rice milk**
- **1/8 tsp (1 ml) fine sea salt**
- **1 Tbsp (15 ml) pure vanilla extract**

In the bowl of a food processor, blend the potato starch, cocoa, coconut oil, and 1/4 cup (40 g) of the cornstarch until you have a smooth and creamy mixture that looks like regular frosting. Be sure to scrape the sides and bottom of the bowl, lifting the blades to scrape under them, to ensure that all the starch and cocoa are incorporated. Set aside.

In a small, heavy bottomed pot, whisk together the agave nectar and last 1/4 cup (40 g) cornstarch until well blended and smooth (mixing the cornstarch with the agave first will help prevent lumps from forming when the frosting is cooked). Slowly add the rice milk and salt and whisk again until smooth. Heat the mixture over medium heat, stirring constantly, until it begins to bubble around the edges of the pan, about 5 minutes. Lower heat and stir for another 1 minute, or until the mixture resembles a thick caramel sauce. Remove from heat and stir in the vanilla.

Scrape the hot mixture right into the processor bowl over the cocoa mixture. Process until very well blended and completely smooth, stopping to scrape the sides of the processor if necessary. The mixture will be glossy and thick, with a fudgy, almost gel-like texture. Turn the frosting into a deep bowl. To use as a fudgy chocolate frosting, allow the mixture to cool to room temperature and spread on desired cake or cupcakes.

To use as a buttercream frosting, place the mixture in the refrigerator until perfectly cold and solid; continue with the steps below.

Once the mixture is cold, remove it from the fridge and loosen it from the sides of the bowl with a spoon or heavy plastic spatula. Then, beat the frosting with electric beaters until fluffy, 3-5 minutes. It may look at first as if you have a curdled, separated mass of dark goop, but if you keep beating, the mixture should begin to lighten up, both in color and texture, and become fluffy. If the frosting is too thick, add more rice milk, *one teaspoon at a time*, and beat again. (Resist the temptation to add more milk at one time; this frosting can transform from being too thick to being too thin really quickly).

Once the mixture is fluffy, you can spread it directly onto a cake or cupcakes, or pipe it. Store in the refrigerator for up to one week and remove about 20 minutes before serving.

Makes enough for top and sides of one 9" cake (one layer) or 9 cupcakes.

> **Note:** You can certainly use unrefined coconut oil in this recipe, but the frosting will have a distinct coconut flavor.

Gluten Free, Sugar Free, Soy Free Pastry Cream

GF NF SF

Years ago at a cooking class, I tasted pastry cream for the first time. Immediately smitten, I continued to use egg and cream based, sugary filling as a staple in fruit tarts for many years. When my diet changed, I thought I'd given up this rich, creamy filling—until now. It takes some time and work, but the results are worth it for a sugar-free, egg-free, butter-free pastry cream this good!

1/4 cup (50 g) dry millet

1/2 cup (120 ml) water, or plain or vanilla rice milk

1 can (14 oz. or 400 ml) full-fat coconut milk

Pinch fine sea salt

1/3 cup (80 ml) light agave nectar

1 Tbsp (15 ml) pure vanilla extract

1/4 tsp (1 ml) pure almond extract (optional)

1 Tbsp (15 ml) cornstarch, if necessary (see note)

Place the millet and water or rice milk in a medium pot and bring to boil; lower heat to simmer, cover, and cook until the liquid is completely absorbed, about 15-20 minutes.

Add the coconut milk, salt and agave nectar, and return to boil over medium heat. Lower heat to simmer once more and continue to cook, stirring frequently to avoid scorching (I find a silicon spatula works beautifully for this, as you can scrape clean the bottom of the pot), until the liquid is almost absorbed, the grains of millet have begun to break open and disintegrate into the liquid, and the mixture has a texture of thick wallpaper paste (or very thick oatmeal), 30-40 minutes. If necessary, add a bit more water, about 1/4 cup (60 ml) at a time, to ensure that the mixture has cooked long enough (don't worry about overcooking at this point—the longer it cooks, the better!).

Remove from heat; stir in the vanilla and almond extract and cool for a couple of minutes.

Pour the mixture in 1/2 cup (120 ml) batches into a powerful blender (**a hand blender or food processor is not suitable for this recipe**) and blend, scraping down sides of blender repeatedly, until the mixture is perfectly smooth and velvety. (Using my conventional blender, I had to stop and scrape the sides about 10-15 times to achieve this result). Turn each batch into the bowl once smooth, and continue until all the mixture has been blended and poured into the bowl. Use immediately or refrigerate for later use.

Spread the smooth pastry cream over pie crust, or use as a custard in a parfait, tarts, or as a filling for a layer cake. Makes enough for one large pie or tart, or filling for 10-12 cupcakes.

> **Note:** if you find that the blended pastry cream is too thin, add the cornstarch and blend again. It should thicken up as it sits.

Golden Vanilla Cake

Sweetened only with agave nectar, this vanilla cake resembles a traditional "yellow" cake. This is a moist and light cake that's perfect baked in layers for a special occasion, or divided into golden, domed cupcakes as individual treats.

3 Tbsp (15 g) finely ground flax seeds

3/4 cup plus 2 Tbsp (210 ml) light agave nectar

3/4 cup (180 ml) vanilla soy or almond milk

1/3 cup (80 ml) sunflower or other light-tasting oil, preferably organic

2 Tbsp (30 ml) pure vanilla extract

2 tsp (10 ml) apple cider vinegar

2 cups (280 g) light spelt flour

1-1/2 tsp (7.5 ml) baking powder

1 tsp (5 ml) baking soda

1/2 tsp (2.5 ml) fine sea salt

Preheat oven to 350F (180C). Line two 8-inch (20 cm) round layer pans with parchment paper, or spray with nonstick spray.

In a medium bowl, whisk together the flax seeds, agave nectar, soymilk, oil, vanilla and vinegar. Set aside while you measure the dry ingredients, or at least 2 minutes.

In a large bowl, sift together the flour, baking powder, soda and salt. Pour the wet mixture over the dry and whisk again to combine; do not overmix.

Divide the batter evenly between the two pans (you can weigh it, or just estimate by setting the pans side by side on a counter as you pour and aiming for equal levels).

Bake in preheated over for 35-40 minutes, rotating the pans about halfway through, until a tester inserted in the center of each pan comes out clean (depending on where they were situated in the oven, the two layers may not be ready at exactly the same time). Cool in pan at least 15 minutes before cutting.

If you will be frosting the cake, this works best if you freeze the cake for an hour or two first, then remove from the pan and frost while still frozen, as this helps prevent crumbling (the cake is quite delicate otherwise). Frost as desired. Makes 8-10 servings. May be frozen (depending on frosting used).

Variation: for cupcakes, line 24 cupcake cups with paper liners, or spray with nonstick spray. Bake 20-25 minutes, until a tester inserted in one of the center cupcakes comes out clean. Cool 5 minutes in pan before removing to a rack to cool completely.

Holiday Apple Cake

A cake this big and bursting with apples really does evoke a celebration. My mom used to bake a similar cake for the holidays in our house. With its double layer of cinnamon-soaked apples and moist, honeyed cake, this beauty will likely become a favorite at your house, too.

3-1/2 to 4 cups (about 800 ml) thinly sliced apple (from about 4 large, peeled and cored apples; or leave the peel on if you prefer)

1/4 cup (45 g) Sucanat (or other unrefined evaporated cane juice)

2 tsp (10 ml) cinnamon

1/2 cup (120 ml) light agave nectar

1/4 cup (60 ml) brown rice syrup

2 tsp (10 ml) finely ground chia seeds

1/3 cup (80 ml) sunflower or other light-tasting oil, preferably organic

3/4 cup (180 ml) plain or vanilla soy or almond milk

1 Tbsp (15 ml) pure vanilla extract

2 tsp (10 ml) apple cider vinegar

1/2 tsp (2.5 ml) pure lemon extract

1-1/2 cups (215 g) light spelt flour

3/4 cup (90 g) barley flour

1 Tbsp (15 ml) baking powder

1 tsp (5 ml) baking soda

1/2 tsp (2.5 ml) fine sea salt

Preheat oven to 350F (180C). Lightly grease a large bundt pan with coconut oil or spray with nonstick spray.

In a medium bowl, toss the apple slices with the Sucanat and cinnamon; set aside.

In another medium bowl, combine the agave nectar, brown rice syrup, chia seeds, oil, soymilk, vanilla, vinegar and lemon extract. Whisk together to ensure that there are no small lumps of chia visible. Set aside while you measure the dry ingredients, or at least 2 minutes.

In a large bowl, sift together the spelt flour, barley flour, baking powder, baking soda and salt. Pour the wet mixture over the dry and stir to blend.

Pour 1/3 of the batter into the bottom of the pan (you can just estimate). Cover with a layer of about 1/2 the apples, taking care not to let apples touch the sides of the pan (it's not a tragedy if they do happen to touch the sides, but it will make it a bit more difficult to remove the cake from the pan without it breaking). Top with another 1/3 of the batter, gently spreading to cover the apples as completely as possible. Add the rest of the apples, again taking care not to touch the sides of the pan; finish with the last 1/3 of the batter, and gently smooth the top. All the apples should be covered with batter; if a tiny edge or point of apple sticks out from the batter on top, this is fine, but most should be under batter.

Bake in preheated oven for 50 to 60 minutes, rotating pan about halfway through, until a tester inserted halfway between the outside and inside walls of the pan comes out clean (it can be moist from the apples, but shouldn't have any batter on it). The cake will be domed on top and deep golden.

Allow the cake to cool in the pan for 20 minutes before turning out onto a rack and cooling completely. This cake is lovely plain, with ice cream or whipped cream (recipe, page 125), or dusted with some Sucanat and cinnamon that have been powdered in a blender or coffee grinder. Makes up to 24 servings. Store covered in refrigerator for up to 5 days. May be frozen.

Light Lemony Buttercream Frosting

A light airy frosting with subtle lemon flavor is perfect for delicate cakes or cupcakes. You can create variations by replacing the lemon flavoring with orange or almond.

1/3 cup (70 g) refined coconut oil, preferably organic (see note 1)
1/4 cup (45 g) potato starch
6 Tbsp (60 g) organic cornstarch, divided
1/3 cup (80 ml) light agave nectar
1/4 cup (60 ml) vanilla soy, almond, or rice milk
Pinch fine sea salt
1 tsp (5 ml) very finely grated lemon zest
1/2 tsp (2.5 ml) pure lemon extract (optional)
2 tsp (10 ml) pure vanilla extract

In the bowl of a food processor, combine the coconut oil, potato starch and 4 Tbsp (40 g) of the cornstarch and blend to a thick paste. Be sure to scrape the sides and bottom of the bowl, lifting the blades to scrape under them, to ensure that all the starch is incorporated. Set aside.

In a small, heavy-bottomed pot, whisk together the agave nectar and last 2 Tbsp (20 g) cornstarch until smooth (mixing the agave with the cornstarch first prevents lumps from forming when the frosting is cooked). Slowly add the soymilk until blended, then add the salt. Using a silicon spatula or whisk, cook over medium heat, stirring constantly, until the mixture begins to thicken and become clear, about 5 minutes. Continue to cook and stir for about 30 seconds (it may bubble a bit), scraping the bottom with the whisk or spatula to ensure it doesn't scorch. The mixture should be golden and almost gel-like, with a texture similar to lemon curd. Remove from heat and stir in the lemon extract and vanilla.

Add the hot agave mixture to the processor bowl and blend again, scraping sides if necessary, until everything is incorporated into a smooth and slightly gluey consistency (don't worry! It won't stay this way once it's cooled and beaten). Turn the mixture into a deep bowl and refrigerate until cold, 30 minutes to an hour.

Once the frosting is cold, beat it at high speed with electric beaters, scraping sides of bowl frequently, until it begins to lighten in color (turning opaque and white), thicken and become fluffy (2-3 minutes). When you first start to beat it, it may appear curdled and you'll wonder if it will transform in to a spreadable frosting; but keep beating, and it will soften, lighten up and become fluffy (see note 2). Spread on cake or pipe as desired.

Makes enough to frost a single layer or 8-10 cupcakes. Store in refrigerator, but bring to room temperature before serving.

Note 1: You can certainly use unrefined coconut oil in this recipe, but there will be a pronounced coconut flavor.

Note 2: The final thickness of the frosting will depend on the heat of your stove, the pot you used, and the exact time that the frosting was cooked. Because of these slight variations, your final frosting may turn out slightly thicker or slightly thinner than mine.

If you find it is too thick to spread even after it's beaten, try this: add a bit more milk, *one teaspoon at a time*, and beat again until you reach the desired consistency. (Resist the temptation to add more milk at one time; this frosting can transform from being too thick to being too thin really quickly).

If you find it is too thin to spread and is almost pudding-like, try this: return the frosting to the refrigerator until it is very cold. Melt an additional 2 Tbsp (30 ml) coconut oil in a small bowl, and then pour over the cold frosting; beat again to incorporate the coconut oil. The frosting should thicken up nicely.

Variations: Replace lemon extract with orange or almond extract, or 1 tsp (5ml.) instant coffee dissolved in 1 tsp (5 ml) water.

Mrs. K's Date Cake

This is the kind of cake you like to have on hand as an after-school snack, or when you're feeling peckish mid-morning. Baked in a square pan, it will keep, covered on the counter, for up to 4 days, longer if refrigerated (bring to room temperature before indulging).

Cake:
Heaping 1/2 cup (75 g) finely chopped dried unsweetened dates

1 cup (240 ml) boiling water

1/2 cup (90 g) Sucanat (or other unrefined evaporated cane juice)

2 Tbsp (30 ml) finely ground flax seeds

1/4 cup (60 ml) unsweetened coconut milk, almond milk or soymilk

1/4 cup (60 ml) sunflower or other light-tasting oil, preferably organic

2 tsp (10 ml) pure vanilla extract

1 cup plus 3 Tbsp (170 g) light spelt flour

1 heaping Tbsp (15 ml) dark cocoa powder (preferably not Dutch process)

1/2 tsp (2.5 ml) baking powder

1/2 tsp (2.5 ml) baking soda

1/4 tsp (1 ml) fine sea salt

Topping:
2 Tbsp (30 ml) Sucanat (or other unrefined evaporated cane juice)

1/4 cup (20 g) unsweetened shredded coconut

1/2 cup (100 g) dairy-free dark chocolate chips

Make the cake: Preheat oven to 350F (180C). Line an 8-1/2" (21 cm) square pan with parchment paper, or spray with nonstick spray.

Place the dates in a medium bowl and pour the boiling water over them; stir briefly. Add the 1/2 cup (90 g) Sucanat, flax seeds, coconut milk, oil and vanilla, and stir to blend. Allow the mixture to sit until it reaches room temperature, about 15 minutes.

Meanwhile, in a large bowl sift together the flour, cocoa, baking powder, baking soda and salt. Pour the cooled wet mixture over the dry and stir to blend. Turn into the prepared pan and smooth the top.

Sprinkle the topping ingredients over the cake: first, sprinkle the 2 Tbsp (30 ml) Sucanat evenly over the surface of the batter. Cover with a sprinkling of the coconut, and end with the chocolate chips.

Bake for 35-40 minutes, rotating pan about halfway through, until a tester inserted in the center of the cake come out clean. Allow to cool in the pan for at least 20 minutes before cutting (if you cut this cake while it's still warm, the still-melty chips will cling to the knife and you will end up with a blob of goo instead of a piece of cake). Makes 9 large or 12 medium-sized pieces. May be frozen.

Pear Upside Down Cake

A newfangled version of an upside-down cake without the usual sugary, sticky fruit topping (or is that "bottom"?).

Filling and Topping:
4 medium pears, peeled, cored, and sliced thin
2/3 cup (75 g) chopped walnuts or pecans, or pieces
1-1/2 tsp (7.5 ml) cinnamon
sprinkling of pure maple syrup (optional)

Batter:
2 cups (280 g) light spelt flour
1 Tbsp (15 ml) baking powder
1/4 tsp (1 ml) fine sea salt
1/4 cup (60 ml) packed silken tofu
1/2 cup (120 ml) light agave nectar
1/3 cup (80 ml) sunflower or other light-tasting oil, preferably organic
Grated zest of one lemon
1/2 cup (120 ml) plain or vanilla soymilk or almond milk

Preheat oven to 350F (180C). Line a 9" (22.5 cm) square pan with parchment paper and spray sides with nonstick spray (**the parchment on the bottom is essential for this cake**).

Make the topping: In a bowl, combine pears, walnuts, cinnamon, and maple syrup, if desired. Mix well to coat pears with cinnamon. Sprinkle about half the topping in the bottom of the prepared pan, distributing the nuts evenly.

Prepare the batter: In a large bowl, sift together the flour, baking powder and salt. Set aside.

In a food processor, blend the tofu and agave nectar until smooth and no pieces of tofu are visible. Add the oil, lemon zest and soymilk and process to combine. Pour over dry ingredients and mix well.

Spread half the batter evenly over topping in pan. Sprinkle remaining pear mixture over top, then cover with remaining batter and smooth the top (it's okay if the batter doesn't quite cover every spot on the top of the filling; smooth it over as best you can).

Bake in preheated oven 40-50 minutes, rotating pan about halfway through, until a tester inserted in center of cake comes out clean.

Cool 10 minutes, then turn out onto a platter or wire rack. Peel off parchment and scrape any topping that sticks to paper, returning it to the top of the cake. Spread top smooth if necessary. Allow to cool completely before cutting into 12 or 16 pieces. May be frozen.

Variation: Substitute apples, peaches, or pineapple for the pears.

Plum-Topped Cornmeal Cake

I actually wavered a bit when trying to decide the chapter in which I'd include this cake: is it a dessert, or a breakfast treat? Neither too sweet nor too delicate, this cake is perfect for either one—or anything in between!

Cake:

10-12 small fresh, ripe purple or red plums (not the European prune variety), cut in half and pitted

1 Tbsp (15 ml) finely ground flax seeds

Finely grated zest of one small orange

Juice of one small orange plus enough plain or vanilla soy or almond milk to equal 3/4 cup (180 ml) liquid

1/3 cup (80 ml) agave nectar, light or dark

1/4 cup (60 ml) sunflower or other light-tasting oil, preferably organic

1-3/4 cups (245 g) light spelt flour

3/4 cup (135 g) cornmeal, preferably organic

1 Tbsp (15 ml) baking powder

1/4 tsp (1.5 ml) baking soda

1/4 tsp (1 ml) fine sea salt

Optional Glaze:

1 Tbsp (15 ml) light agave nectar

1 Tbsp (15 ml) water

Make the cake: Preheat oven to 350 F (180 C). Lightly grease a flan pan or 9" (22.5 cm) springform pan with coconut oil, or spray with nonstick spray.

Cut each plum in half and remove the pit. Place skin down on a plate or cutting board.

In a medium bowl, mix the flax seeds, orange juice-soymilk mixture, zest, 1/3 cup (80 ml) agave nectar and oil. Whisk to blend and set aside while you measure the dry ingredients, or at least 2 minutes.

In a large bowl, sift the flour, cornmeal, baking powder, baking soda, and salt. Pour the wet mixture over the dry and mix to combine. Turn the batter into the prepared pan and smooth the top.

Place the plum halves skin side down over the surface of the batter in a decorative arrangement. Press the plums into the batter slightly.

Bake for 25 minutes, then glaze the top if desired (prepare the glaze while cake is baking). Rotate the pan and return the cake to the oven for another 10 minutes or so, until the top is golden and the cake part tests done when a tester is inserted into it. Serve warm or at room temperature. Makes 10 servings.

While the cake bakes, make the glaze: combine the 1 Tbsp (15 ml) agave nectar and water in a small bowl; brush over surface of cooled cake.

> **Variation:** If you prefer cornmeal-plum muffins, use only 4-5 plums and chop them after removing the pits; fold the plums into the batter before spooning into prepared muffin tins instead of the flan pan (and bake for 20-25 minutes, until a tester inserted in the middle of a center muffin comes out clean).

Soy Free, Sugar Free Coconut Whipped "Cream"

In creating this recipe, I ended up testing it more than 50 times—by far the most in the entire book— and am happy to say I'm thrilled with this final version. It's a slightly fussy recipe with several steps, but the result is well worth the effort: you'll have a light, creamy, fluffy topping that can be piped or plopped in dollops atop shortcake or pie, all without soy or sugar.

- **1-1/2 level tsp (7.5 ml) agar powder or 1 level Tbsp plus 1 level tsp (30 ml) agar flakes**
- **2 Tbsp (30 ml) organic cornstarch, divided (arrowroot won't work for this recipe)**
- **3 Tbsp (45 ml) light agave nectar**
- **1/3 cup (80 ml) plain or vanilla rice or almond milk**
- **1 14-ounce (400 ml) can full-fat coconut milk (I use Thai Kitchen; the higher the total fat content, the better), at room temperature; shake well before opening**
- **1/8 tsp (.5 ml) fine sea salt**
- **2 tsp (10 ml) pure vanilla extract**
- **1-2 Tbsp (15-30 ml) coconut oil, preferably organic, melted (optional; will depend on the fat content of the coconut milk)**

For agar powder: In a small bowl, combine the agar powder, 1 Tbsp (15 ml) cornstarch and agave nectar. Whisk well to eliminate any lumps.

Pour the coconut milk, rice milk and salt into a small heavy pot. Slowly whisk in the agave mixture until well combined.

Heat the mixture over medium heat, stirring constantly, until it begins to boil. Continue stirring constantly and cooking over medium heat for one minute. Remove from heat and stir in the vanilla.

Pour the mixture into a deep bowl. Allow to cool to room temperature, about 30 minutes, stirring once every minute for the first 5 minutes. Place the bowl in the refrigerator and allow to chill completely, at least 4 hours.

For agar flakes: Combine agar, rice or almond milk, coconut milk and salt in a small, heavy bottomed pot; allow to sit at room temperature, covered, for at least 20 minutes to soften the agar.

In a small bowl, whisk together 1 Tbsp cornstarch and agave nectar until smooth. Add to the agar-milk mixture in the pot and stir to blend.

Heat the mixture over medium heat, stirring constantly, until it begins to boil. Reduce heat to low and continue cooking and stirring for 5 minutes, scraping the bottom of the pot occasionally to avoid scorching. Remove from heat and stir in the vanilla.

Strain the mixture through a fine sieve into a deep bowl (this will catch any bits of flakes that haven't dissolved entirely; you definitely don't want chunks of agar in your whipped cream!). Allow to cool to room temperature, about 30 minutes, stirring once every minute for the first 5 minutes. Place the bowl in the refrigerator and allow to chill completely, no less than 4 hours.

Once chilled, proceed as follows for both agar powder and agar flakes: Break the chilled mixture into large chunks (it should be jelled and quite solid) and place in a food processor. Sprinkle with the last 1 Tbsp (15 ml) cornstarch and process until perfectly smooth, stopping to scrape down sides two or three times. The mixture should have no visible little lumps or grains of gel, and should be very fluffy and smooth. At this point, the cream may be used as is to dollop over pies or puddings. For a firmer cream that can be piped, continue as below.

If the cream is not quite stiff enough to pipe, beat it with electric beaters, as follows: turn the already-processed cream into a deep bowl. If you have time, refrigerate for another 10-15 minutes until very cold (otherwise, place the beaters in the freezer for a few minutes). Melt the coconut oil (start with one Tbsp or 15 ml). While beating the cream, pour the melted oil in a stream over it, and beat on high speed to incorporate; the cold cream and beaters will help to congeal the oil as it's blended in. The cream should thicken enough to hold a shape. If necessary, use the final Tbsp (15 ml) of oil as well.

Store in refrigerator up to 5 days. The cream will keep its shape and should still remain soft. Makes about 2 cups (500 ml).

Tomato Spice Cake

This cake is modeled on one my mother used to bake when I was a child. She used canned tomato soup in her batter as well as white sugar and flour—but I think this version is as good, if not better tasting! Don't be afraid of the tomato in here—it's not discernible and the cake tastes like a regular spice cake (and tomatoes are fruits, after all!).

- **1 large tomato, about 6-1/2 ounces (190 g), hard stem section cut off (but you can leave the skin on)**
- **1/3 cup (60 g) Sucanat (or other unrefined evaporated cane juice)**
- **1/4 cup (60 ml) agave nectar, light or dark**
- **3/8 cup (6 Tbsp or 90 ml) plain or vanilla rice milk**
- **1/4 cup (60 ml) sunflower or other light-tasting oil, preferably organic**
- **1-1/2 tsp (7.5 ml) finely ground chia seeds**
- **1/2 cup (70 g) raisins**
- **1-1/2 cups plus 2 Tbsp (230 g) light spelt flour**
- **2 tsp (10 ml) baking powder**
- **1/2 tsp (2.5 ml) baking soda**
- **1 tsp (5 ml) ground cinnamon**
- **1/2 tsp (2.5 ml) ground nutmeg**
- **1/4 tsp (1 ml) ground ginger**
- **1/4 tsp (1 ml) fine sea salt**

Preheat oven to 350F (180C). Line an 8" (20 cm) square pan with parchment paper, or spray with nonstick spray.

Wash the tomato and cut into eighths. Place the chunks in a food processor and process until you have a smooth purée (it will be very watery; this is as it should be). Add the Sucanat, agave nectar, rice milk, oil and chia seeds. Process again until everything is well combined and no lumps of chia remain. Add the raisins and stir by hand to coat, but don't process again. Set aside.

In a large bowl, sift together the flour, baking powder, baking soda, cinnamon, nutmeg, ginger and salt. Pour the wet ingredients over the dry and stir to mix well.

Spread the batter in the prepared pan and smooth the top. Bake in preheated oven 25-35 minutes, rotating pan about halfway through, until the top is rounded and a tester inserted in the center comes out clean but moist. Cool at least 10 minutes before attempting to cut. Makes 9 large or 12 more reasonable pieces. May be frozen.

Vanilla Pastry Cream or Buttercream Frosting

This wonderfully versatile frosting and filling can be used with fruit in tarts, as a filling in cakes or pies, or as a frosting in its own right. I like it contrasted between chocolate layers when the rest of the cake is frosted with chocolate.

6 Tbsp (80 g) refined coconut oil, preferably organic (see note 1)

2 Tbsp (30 ml) organic cornstarch

Pinch fine sea salt

1/3 cup (80 ml) light agave nectar

5 Tbsp (40 g) light spelt flour

1/2 cup (120 ml) plain or vanilla soy, almond or rice milk

1 Tbsp (15 ml) pure vanilla extract (if using vanilla milk) OR 1 Tbsp plus 1 tsp (20 ml) pure vanilla extract (if using plain milk)

In the bowl of a food processor, combine the coconut oil, cornstarch and salt and blend to a paste. Be sure to scrape the sides and bottom of the bowl, lifting the blades to scrape under them, to ensure that all the starch is incorporated. Set aside.

In a small, heavy-bottomed pot, whisk together the agave nectar and flour until very smooth and no lumps are visible. Slowly add the soymilk until blended. (Blending the agave with the flour first helps to eliminate any lumps that might form when the frosting is cooked).

Now, get ready for some muscle power! Using a silicon spatula or whisk, cook over medium heat, stirring constantly, until the mixture begins to thicken; it will thicken on the bottom of the pot fairly quickly, and you'll need to stir vigorously to prevent clumps from forming. Reduce heat to medium-low and continue to cook and stir for one minute, scraping the bottom with the whisk or spatula to ensure it doesn't scorch, until the mixture is uniformly thick and attains the texture of a thick paste. Remove from heat and stir in the vanilla (it should be too thick to use as frosting at this point).

Add the hot agave mixture to the processor bowl and blend again, scraping sides if necessary, until everything comes together in a thick, glossy spread. (If it refuses to come together and the oil separates out, add more soymilk, *one teaspoon at a time*, and blend again until it reaches this texture. Resist the temptation to add more milk at one time; this frosting can transform from being too thick to being too thin really quickly.) It should have a slightly golden color and be thick enough to hold its shape.

To use as a pastry cream, pour the mixture as is into a tart or pie shell, or spread between cake layers.

For a lighter frosting with a buttercream texture, pour the mixture into a deep bowl and refrigerate until very cold (at least an hour).

Once cold, beat the frosting with electric beaters at high speed, scraping sides of bowl frequently, until it turns a shade or two lighter (it will become opaque and white), thickens and becomes fluffy (2-3 minutes). When you first start to beat it, it will remain thick and light golden, and you may wonder if it will transform in to a spreadable frosting; but keep beating, and it will soften and lighten up, becoming fluffy (see note 2). Once beaten, spread the frosting on a cake or cupcakes, or pipe as desired.

Makes enough to frost a single layer or 8-10 cupcakes. Store in refrigerator, but bring to room temperature before serving. May be frozen (defrost overnight in a covered container in the refrigerator, then beat again before using).

Note 1: You can certainly use unrefined coconut oil in this recipe, but there will be a pronounced coconut flavor.

Note 2: The final thickness of the frosting will depend on the exact heat of your stove, the pot you used, and the exact time that the frosting was cooked. Because of these slight variations, your final frosting may turn out slightly thicker or slightly thinner than mine.

If you find it is too thick to spread even after it's beaten, try this: add a bit more milk, *one teaspoon at a time*, and beat again until you reach the desired consistency. (Resist the temptation to add more milk at one time; this frosting can transform from being too thick to being too thin really quickly).

If you find it is too thin to spread and is almost pudding-like, try this: return the frosting to the refrigerator until it is very cold. Melt an additional 2 Tbsp (30 ml) coconut oil in a small bowl, and then pour over the cold frosting; beat again to incorporate the coconut oil. The frosting should thicken up nicely and become fluffy.

Variations: Reduce vanilla to 1 tsp (5 ml) and add 1 tsp (5 ml) lemon, orange, almond or coffee extract.

"CHEESECAKES,"

PIES and

BAKED PUDDINGS

Berries and Cream Tart

recipe, page 135

Chocolate Pecan Pie

recipe, page 140

My Mother's Cheesecake

recipe, page 143

Cheesecakes, Pies, and Baked Puddings

I have to admit I've never been much of a pie person. Oh, I like them well enough if someone else goes to the trouble of making a crust and baking it; but I'd never been successful at fashioning my own pastry from scratch in the past. Once I finally stopped using conventional ingredients in my pie crusts, however, I fell in love!

Unlike most crusts, those featured here don't require pre-chilling or even rolling. And some are made from ground nuts, which confers a rich, sandy texture reminiscent of shortbread in a crust that holds up beautifully when filled.

In this chapter, you'll find a variety of pies and tarts as well as a few rich and creamy "cheesecakes" and baked puddings. While the Gluten Free Berries and Cream Tart boasts a pastry cream filling made from (for the most part) millet, most of the creamy or cheesecake-like fillings in this chapter do contain tofu. If you're avoiding soy, opt for the very decadent Chocolate Pecan Pie, the Chocolate Satin Tarts (rich chocolate ganache nestled in a chocolate shortbread crust), or the classic Canadian treat, Butter Tarts (without eggs, dairy, or sugar, of course).

For classic baked puddings, there's an easy Banana Bread Pudding with Warm Maple Syrup and Spiced Pumpkin Millet Pudding, a comforting winter treat.

Whether or not you're a pie person, too, you'll find plenty of rich, delicious treats in this chapter!

Banana Bread Pudding and Warm Maple Custard Sauce

You could just as easily use this recipe for vegan French Toast: omit cherries and maple syrup, mix all ingredients except bread in a bowl, dip bread slices in the mixture and fry until golden in a nonstick pan. Either way, this is a satisfying, delicious comfort food!

For the bread pudding:
6-8 slices of your favorite wheat-free bread (I use spelt or kamut sourdough)

1 very ripe, medium-sized banana

2 cups (480 ml) plain or vanilla soy, almond or rice milk (see note)

1 tsp (5 ml) pure vanilla extract

1/3 cup (80 ml) pure maple syrup

1/4 tsp (1 ml) ground nutmeg

1 tsp (5 ml) ground cinnamon

1-1/2 tsp (7.5 ml) arrowroot powder or organic cornstarch

1 Tbsp (15 ml) finely ground flax seeds

1/2-2/3 cup (60-80 g) dried tart cherries, dried cranberries or raisins

For the Custard Sauce:
1 cup (240 ml) plain or vanilla soy, almond or rice milk

2 Tbsp (30 ml) organic cornstarch or arrowroot powder

1/4 cup (60 ml) pure maple syrup

1 tsp (5 ml) pure vanilla extract

Preheat oven to 350F (180C). Line a 9" (22.5 cm) square pan or soufflé dish with parchment paper, or spray with nonstick spray.

Make the pudding: Tear bread into bite-sized pieces and place in a large bowl.

Combine all other bread pudding ingredients except cherries in a blender or food processor and blend until smooth. Pour over bread in bowl and add cherries. Turn the mixture into the prepared pan and press down with a wooden spoon or spatula so that all pieces are covered in liquid. Let sit about 15 minutes.

Bake in preheated oven about 40 minutes, rotating pan about halfway through, until puffed and golden brown on top. Let cool slightly before slicing or spooning onto plates. Spoon warm custard sauce over top. Makes 8-10 servings.

As the pudding bakes, make the custard sauce: Combine cornstarch and about 1/4 cup (60 ml) of the soymilk in a small bowl and mix well. Pour the remainder of the soymilk and 1/4 cup (60 ml) maple syrup into a small, heavy pot. Add the cornstarch mixture and whisk to combine.

Cook over medium heat, stirring constantly, until mixture comes to a boil. Continue to cook and stir until mixture is thickened, 30 seconds to one minute. Remove from heat and add the 1 tsp (5 ml) vanilla. Let cool slightly before drizzling over bread pudding.

Note: for a richer pudding, use half soy or almond milk and half coconut milk.

Berries and Cream Tart

GF NF SF

This tart makes a spectacular summer dessert. It takes a bit of planning to make the cream in advance, but once you've got the parts mixed up, it's a snap to assemble. And your guests will be very impressed!

1 recipe Gluten Free, Sugar Free, Soy Free Pastry Cream (page 117)

1 prebaked pie crust (use the recipe on page 138 if gluten isn't a problem , a bought crust or gluten-free crust for GF version)

About 2 cups (480 ml) fresh mixed berries, such as sliced strawberries, raspberries and blueberries

1 recipe Glaze (below).

Make the pastry cream: mix up a batch of pastry cream and allow to cool to room temperature.

Meanwhile, prepare the pie crust: if baking it from scratch, prebake and allow to cool.

Sort and wash your berries; dry on paper towels.

Assemble the tart: Spread the pastry cream evenly over the cooled pie crust. Place the berries in a decorative pattern over the pastry cream, leaving as little space between berries as possible. Refrigerate while you make the glaze. Once glaze has cooled, brush it gently over the surface of the berries, allowing it to drip between the berries over the top of the tart. Makes 10-12 servings. Store, covered, in the refrigerator for up to 5 days.

For glaze: In a small bowl, whisk together 1/4 cup (60 ml) light agave nectar and 2 tsp (10 ml) organic cornstarch until smooth. Pour 1/2 cup (120 ml) water into a small, heavy pot, and slowly whisk in the agave mixture. Bring to boil over medium heat and boil for 30 seconds, stirring constantly. Allow to cool for at least 10 minutes before brushing on the tart.

Butter Tarts, Glorious and Free (of Eggs and Dairy)

In Ontario, where I live, butter tarts are the quintessential Canadian dessert. Much like a pecan pie without the pecans, the traditional butter tarts are rich and gooey with butter, eggs and lots of sugar. Here's my adapted version, every bit as delectable, but so much kinder to your health!

Crust:
1-2/3 cups (220 g) whole spelt flour
1/4 tsp (1 ml) fine sea salt
1/2 cup (120 ml) coconut oil, preferably organic, melted
2 Tbsp (30 ml) light agave nectar

Filling:
1/4 cup (35 g) raisins
1/2 cup (120 ml) brown rice syrup
1/4 cup (60 ml) light agave nectar
2 Tbsp (30 ml) organic cornstarch
2 Tbsp (30 ml) coconut oil, preferably organic, melted
1 tsp (5 ml) pure vanilla extract
2 tsp (10 ml) brandy or rum (or use another tsp/5 ml vanilla)
2 Tbsp (30 ml) finely ground chia seeds (flax is not suitable for this recipe)
1/4 tsp (1 ml) baking powder

Preheat oven to 325F (165C). Lightly grease 8 individual tart pans (I used 3-inch or 7.5 cm pans with removable bottoms). If you're using solid pans (without removable bottoms), it's worth lining these with parchment paper rounds and then greasing the rounds, as the bottoms may stick to the pan otherwise.

Make the crust: In a medium bowl, sift the flour and salt. Set aside.

In a small bowl, melt the 1/2 cup (120 ml) coconut oil and then whisk in the agave nectar until combined.

Pour the coconut-agave mixture over the flour mixture and toss with a fork until it comes together. Knead with your hands just until the wet ingredients are well incorporated. You should have a very soft dough that just holds its shape (if dough is really too soft, sprinkle more flour, about one Tbsp or 15 ml at a time, until you reach a just barely firm texture--this dough should be *very* soft!). Divide dough into 8 equal portions among the tart pans.

Dust your hands with flour. Beginning with the sides of the tart pans, press the dough evenly to cover each pan; dust hands with flour periodically to prevent the dough from sticking. Place the tart pans on a cookie sheet and bake for 10-12 minutes until the crust is just starting to puff up. Remove from oven and sprinkle about 1/2 Tbsp (7.5 ml) of the raisins in the bottom of each shell (4-6 raisins).

While the crusts bake, make the filling: In a medium bowl, whisk together the brown rice syrup and agave nectar with the cornstarch until the mixture is smooth. Whisk in the melted 2 Tbsp (30 ml) coconut oil, vanilla, brandy and chia seeds (be sure there are no little lumps of chia left in the mixture). Add the baking powder last and mix quickly just to blend.

Divide the mixture equally among the tart pans so the pans are about 3/4 full, or filling is almost even with the top of the crusts (you may have a bit of filling left over--it makes a nice topping over ice cream or pancakes).

Bake 25-30 minutes more in preheated oven, rotating the cookie sheet about halfway through to ensure even baking. The tarts are ready when the filling appears foamy on top and bubbles a little onto the sides of crust in the pans. It will begin to brown on top but will still appear quite liquid when you jiggle the pans; this is as it should be. Remove the tarts carefully from the oven and allow to cool to room temperature, then refrigerate until firm.

These can be eaten cold or at room temperature; for the latter, chill first and then return to room temperature. Store, covered, in the refrigerator for up to 5 days. Makes 8 butter tarts.

Chai Cheesecake

Even though I love the spices in Chai tea, I'm not a fan. In trying to come up with another way to enjoy the spice mix I love, I created this recipe. The fragrant cinnamon, cardamom and ginger are highlighted in this dense, rich, though not too sweet base. This is great served with a big dollop of Coconut Whipped Cream (page 125).

Crust:

1/2 cup (60 g) barley flour

1/4 cup (25 g) ground flax seeds

1/2 cup (50 g) old-fashioned rolled oats (not quick-cooking or instant)

1/2 cup (55 g) walnut pieces or halves

1/4 tsp (1 ml) fine sea salt

2-3 Tbsp (30-45 ml) pure maple syrup

1/4 cup (60 ml) sunflower or other light-tasting oil, preferably organic

Filling:

1 pkg. (1 lb or 425-450 g) firm Chinese-style tofu (the kind in a plastic tub packed in water, *not* individual "bricks" wrapped in plastic or aseptically packaged firm silken tofu)

1/2 cup (120 ml) smooth natural cashew butter, at room temperature

1/3 cup (80 ml) full-fat coconut milk

1/2 cup (120 ml) brown rice syrup

1/2 cup (120 ml) agave nectar, light or dark

2 Tbsp (30 ml) freshly squeezed lemon juice

1 Tbsp (15 ml) pure vanilla extract

1/2 tsp (2.5 ml) pure lemon extract

2 Tbsp (30 ml) organic cornstarch

1 Tbsp (15 ml) carob powder (optional)

2 tsp (10 ml) cinnamon

1 tsp (5 ml) ground ginger

1/4 tsp (1 ml) ground cardamom, more if desired

1/8 tsp (.5 ml) fine sea salt

Make the crust: Preheat oven to 350F (180C). Line the bottom of a 9" (22.5 cm) pie plate with parchment paper, or spray with nonstick spray.

In the bowl of a food processor, combine the flour, flax seeds, rolled oats, walnut pieces and salt and process until you have a fine meal about the texture of cornmeal (there shouldn't be any detectable pieces of nuts in the mixture, though you may still see small flakes of oats).

Drizzle the maple syrup and oil over the dry ingredients and pulse a few times just until well-blended and the mixture comes together in a soft dough. It will be a little sticky, but not so sticky as to adhere to your hand when you pat it in the pie plate (if it's too soft or sticky, sprinkle with another 1 Tbsp (15 ml) flour and mix in by hand). Turn the dough into the pie plate, scraping the processor as clean as you can (don't worry about washing it, as you can use it again in a moment).

Press the dough into the prepared pie plate and flute the sides if desired. Dock the crust by poking holes with a fork five or six times across the bottom of the pie. Bake for 10 minutes in preheated oven, until the crust just begins to puff a bit and appears dry on top, then reduce heat to 325F (165C). Fill with cheesecake mixture and bake as directed below.

While the crust bakes, make the filling: In the bowl of a food processor (there's no need to wash it if you've scraped it fairly clean), process the tofu and cashew butter until smooth. Add the remaining ingredients and process again until well combined and perfectly smooth.

Pour the batter into the still-hot pie crust and smooth the top. Reduce oven temperature to 325F (165C) and bake 45-55 minutes more, rotating pan about halfway through, until the cheesecake is firm or just barely jiggles in the middle when you shake the pan.

Allow to cool to room temperature before refrigerating at least 4 hours. Makes 8-10 servings. Serve with Coconut Whipped "Cream" (recipe, page 125), if desired. Pie (without the cream) may be frozen; defrost, covered, in refrigerator overnight.

Chocolate Pecan Pie

While it's not traditional, this pecan pie is everything a gooey, rich, and decadent treat should be. You'll love the combination of toffee-like filling with chocolate and toasted pecans. This is great for your holiday--or any--table.

Crust:

1/4 cup (60 ml) coconut oil, preferably organic

2 Tbsp (30 ml) sunflower or other light-tasting oil, preferably organic

2 tsp (10 ml) pure maple syrup

1 Tbsp (15 ml) water

1-1/2 cups (210 g) light spelt flour

1/4 tsp (1 ml) baking soda

1/2 tsp (2.5 ml) fine sea salt

Filling:

2/3 cup (160 ml) pure maple syrup

1/3 cup (80 ml) barley malt syrup, brown rice syrup, or any combination of the two that equals 1/3 cup (80 ml) total

2 Tbsp (30 ml) smooth natural cashew butter, at room temperature

3/4 cup (150 g) dairy-free dark chocolate chips

1/8 tsp (.5 ml) fine sea salt

1 Tbsp (15 ml) organic cornstarch or arrowroot powder

1 tsp (5 ml) pure vanilla extract

1-1/2 cups (120 g) pecan pieces (use broken pecan halves)

1/2 cup (40 g) unbroken pecan halves (about 30), for decoration, if desired

Make the crust: Preheat oven to 375F (190C). Line an 8-1/2" or 9" (22 cm) pie plate with parchment paper, or spray with nonstick spray.

In a small heatproof bowl, melt the coconut oil with the sunflower oil. Whisk in the 2 tsp (10 ml) maple syrup and water and set aside.

In a medium bowl, sift the flour with the baking soda and salt. Pour the oil mixture over the dry ingredients and toss with a fork until it comes together. Use your hands to mix into a firm but still pliable dough.

Starting with the sides of the pie plate, press bits of dough along the edges and then the bottom until evenly distributed (you may need to press fairly hard). Flute the edges if you wish, or press with the tines of a fork. Dock the crust by pricking the bottom 10-12 times with a fork.

Bake in preheated oven 20-30 minutes, rotating pan about halfway through, until edges are browned and the rest of the crust is golden. Remove from the oven and pour the hot filling into the crust.

While the crust bakes, make the filling: In a medium, heavy-bottomed pot, combine the 2/3 cup (160 ml) maple syrup, barley malt and/or brown rice syrup, cashew butter, chocolate chips and salt. Cook and stir over medium heat until everything is melted and the mixture is smooth. Sprinkle with the arrowroot powder and whisk to combine.

Continue to cook the mixture, stirring constantly, until the mixture bubbles and boils, 5-10 minutes. Once boiling, reduce heat to medium-low (high enough to keep the mixture boiling, but low enough that it doesn't boil over the top of the pot), and cook for 10-15 more minutes, stirring frequently and scraping the bottom of the pot to prevent scorching. The filling should become thicker and glossy, with a texture similar to corn syrup or molasses. Turn off heat and add the vanilla, then stir in the broken pecan pieces to coat. Pour the hot mixture into the baked pie crust and smooth the top if necessary.

If you'd like to decorate the pie with the unbroken pecan halves, now is the time to do so, while the filling is still hot. Place the halves in a decorative pattern over the filling and press slightly so they adhere to the surface. Allow pie to cool completely at room temperature; then refrigerate until ready to serve. Makes 8-12 slices. May be frozen.

Note: The pie may be eaten cold (straight out of the fridge), but it's best when left at room temperature for 15-20 minutes before serving. Use a long, sharp knife that you dip in hot water and dry between cuts for easier slicing.

Chocolate Satin Tarts

Filled with a smooth, velvety chocolate ganache, these tarts are a wonderfully rich indulgence. Top with some fresh raspberries for a beautiful dessert presentation.

Tart Shells:

1 recipe Chocolate Shortbread dough (recipe, page 80)

Ganache Filling:

10-1/2 ounces (300 g) chopped bittersweet (70% cocoa) chocolate (see note)

1/2 cup (120 ml) full-fat coconut milk (see note)

3 Tbsp (45 ml) pure maple syrup

1/2 tsp (2.5 ml) pure vanilla extract

1 Tbsp (15 ml) cocoa powder, preferably not Dutch process, for dusting tops (optional)

Make the tart shells: Preheat oven to 350F (180C). Lightly grease 8 individual tart pans (I used 3-inch or 7.5 cm pans with removable bottoms). If you're using solid pans (without removable bottoms), it's worth lining these with parchment paper rounds and then greasing the rounds, as the bottoms may stick to the pan otherwise.

Prepare the Chocolate Shortbread Cookie dough (page 80) according to recipe directions.

Divide dough into 6 roughly equal portions. Using your fingers and starting with the sides of the tart pans, press one portion of dough evenly on the bottom and sides of each of the tart pans. Dock the bottom of the tarts by pricking two or three times across with the tines of a fork. Place the tart pans on a cookie sheet, spacing them evenly.

Bake the tart shells in the preheated oven for 12-16 minutes, rotating the cookie sheet about halfway through, until the shells are dry on top, puffed a bit, and browned on the edges. Allow to cool completely before filling.

Meanwhile, make the ganache: In a small, heavy-bottomed pot, combine the chocolate, coconut milk and maple syrup. Cook over low heat, scraping the bottom of the pan occasionally to prevent scorching, until the mixture is smooth and all of the chocolate is melted. Remove from heat and stir in the vanilla.

Divide the ganache evenly among the tart shells. Allow to cool completely at room temperature, then refrigerate until the ganache is firm. Garnish with fresh berries or Coconut Whipped "Cream" (page 125), if desired. May be served cold or at room temperature. Makes 6 large tarts.

Note: Chocolate chips work just fine in this recipe if you don't have chocolate bars. Simply use 10-1/2 ounces (300 g) of chips, but reduce the coconut milk to 7 Tbsp (1/4 cup plus 3 Tbsp) or 105 ml.

My Mother's Cheesecake

My dad grew up on a farm, and his grandmother made old-fashioned cheesecake for special occasions. My mom reproduced the recipe as a treat for my dad, and now I've created a new version that's vegan and free of wheat or sugar. We called this "Farmer's Cheesecake" at home, but I think the credit should go to my mom.

Crust:

1/3 cup (80 ml) sunflower or other light-tasting oil, preferably organic

1/3 cup (80 ml) light agave nectar

2 Tbsp (30 ml) plain or vanilla soy or almond milk

1-1/4 tsp (6.5 ml) pure vanilla extract

1 heaping Tbsp (15 ml) organic cornstarch or arrowroot powder

1 scant cup (130 g) whole spelt flour

3/4 cup (80 g) barley flour

Heaping 1/4 tsp (1.5 ml) baking powder

Heaping 1/4 tsp (1.5 ml) baking soda

Heaping 1/4 tsp (1.5 ml) fine sea salt

Filling:

1 pkg. (12 ounces or 375 g) aseptically packaged firm silken Japanese-style tofu (such as Mori-Nu)

1/2 cup (120 ml) smooth natural cashew butter

Grated zest of one lemon

1/2 cup (120 ml) light agave nectar

2 tsp (10 ml) fresh lemon juice

1/2 tsp (2.5 ml) pure lemon extract

1 tsp (5 ml) pure vanilla extract

Pinch fine sea salt

Preheat oven to 350F (180C). Line an 8" (20 cm) square pan with parchment paper, or spray with nonstick spray.

Prepare the crust: In a medium-sized bowl, whisk together the oil, agave nectar, soymilk and vanilla to emulsify. Sift the remaining ingredients over the mixture in the bowl and stir with a wooden spoon to combine to a soft dough (it will be slightly sticky, but firm enough to hold a shape).

Remove about 1/3 of the dough and set aside (you can just estimate). Press the remaining dough evenly into the bottom of the pan with wet fingers or a silicon spatula (the spatula works well to avoid sticking). Set aside.

Make the filling: blend the tofu and cashew butter in a food processor until well combined, scraping down sides if necessary. Add the remaining ingredients and process until perfectly smooth and velvety (there should be no bits of tofu visible).

Pour the filling evenly over the crust in the pan. To smooth the top, grab the pan on opposite sides with your hands and, keeping the bottom of the pan against the surface it's on, quickly rotate it once to the left and then to the right.

Divide the remaining dough in half, then divide each half into 3 equal parts (you'll have 6 balls of dough). Pinching about 1/2 of each ball at a time, roll it between your palms to create a thin rope about 3/8" (just under 1 cm) thick.

Starting at one corner and working diagonally across to the opposite corner of the pan, place ropes of dough next to each other in a straight line from one corner to the other (the dough doesn't necessarily have to be rolled in a single rope that spans the whole distance across the pan–you can line up shorter pieces next to each other). Next, place ropes of dough on either side parallel to the first rope, so you end up with three diagonal lines across the pan. Continue until you have 5 lines in one direction across the pan (shorter lines toward the edges).

Repeat with ropes of dough in the opposite direction, crossing over the first ropes. You should end up with a diagonal criss-cross pattern over the surface of the cheesecake.

Bake the cake in preheated oven for 30-40 minutes, rotating pan about halfway through, until the filling appears firm and the edges of the dough are beginning to brown. Cool completely, then refrigerate until cold (at least 2 hours) before slicing. Makes 9 large or 12 more reasonable servings. May be frozen (defrost, covered, in the refrigerator overnight).

Spiced Pumpkin Millet Pudding

This pudding is rich and creamy enough to serve as a dessert, but nutritious enough to eat for breakfast as a cooked cereal. I love this cold from the refrigerator, but it's also delicious warm.

1/2 cup (100 g) dry millet

1/2 cup (120 ml) plain or vanilla rice, soy or almond milk

1/2 cup (120 ml) water

1 can (12 oz. or 400 ml) full-fat coconut milk

1/2 cup (120 ml) pumpkin purée (fresh, frozen, or canned)

1/4 cup (60 ml) light agave nectar

1/2 tsp (2.5 ml) ground ginger

1 tsp (5 ml) cinnamon

1/4 tsp (1 ml) nutmeg

Preheat oven to 350 (180C). Grease a casserole dish with coconut oil, or spray with nonstick spray.

Place millet, rice milk and water in a saucepan and bring to boil over medium-high heat. Turn off heat. Add the pumpkin and whisk to blend. Add remaining ingredients and stir to combine. Pour the mixture into the prepared casserole dish and cover.

Bake the covered casserole in preheated oven for about an hour, removing the dish every 20 minutes or so to stir the contents, then replace the cover and return to the oven. After an hour, the millet should be well cooked with the grains beginning to break apart; the pudding will still be fairly loose, but a bit more gelatinous than when it began to bake (it will continue to thicken as it cools). Remove the casserole from the oven and allow to sit, uncovered, at least 20 minutes before serving. Stir again before serving.

May be served warm, at room temperature or cold. If desired, top with Coconut Whipped "Cream" (page 125) or Cashew Cream (page 106). Makes 6 servings.

> **Variation:** Use rice or another grain instead of millet; or add raisins to the pudding if you like.

RAW and

NO-BAKE TREATS

Marbled Halvah

recipe, page 155

Raw Frosted

Apricot Raisin Bars

recipe, page 158

Chocolate Covered

Caramels

(Caramel Cup Variation)

recipe, page 150

Raw and No Bake Treats

While I would never call myself a raw foodist, I did study the living foods lifestyle and diet while I was at nutrition school. I was intrigued by the notion that raw foods, especially fruits and vegetables, contain live enzymes that can actually help your body digest the foods themselves more efficiently. While following a raw foods diet for a couple of months, I also discovered that this type of food is quite delicious.

The recipes in this chapter include raw desserts and other cooked treats that don't require baking. Here's where you'll find my own version of one famous raw fruit and nut bar (the easily addictive Cocoa Nibbles), as well as a wonderful raw bar that doubles as an energy bar, Raw Frosted Raisin-Apricot Bars. The candy-like Marbled Halvah is one of my favorite snacks when my energy wanes in late afternoon. And the tart and chewy Fig and Cherry Bars will provide a good percentage of your daily calcium and protein requirements.

Why turn on the oven when you can still enjoy this type of delectable treat without it?

Chocolate Caramels

There's a vegan brand of caramel here in Toronto made with brown rice syrup and sugar. I've enjoyed them on occasion, but found the price far too high to warrant buying them very often. Instead, I vowed to re-create the recipe on my own. Here's the result: I'm pleased to say I haven't bought the other ones since!

Caramels:
1/2 cup pecan (40 g) or walnut (50 g) pieces, lightly toasted

1/2 cup (120 ml) brown rice syrup

1/4 cup (45 g) Sucanat (or other unrefined evaporated cane juice)

2 Tbsp (30 ml) coconut oil, preferably organic

2 Tbsp (30 ml) plain or vanilla soy or almond milk

1/8 tsp (.5 ml) fine sea salt

1 tsp (5 ml) pure vanilla extract

Coating (optional):
1 cup (200 g) dairy free dark chocolate chips

2 tsp (10 ml) coconut oil, preferably organic

Make the caramels: Line an 8" (20 cm) loaf pan with parchment or waxed paper; grease the paper. Sprinkle the nuts evenly in the bottom of the pan. Set aside.

In a small, heavy-bottomed pot, whisk together the rice syrup, Sucanat, 2 Tbsp (30 ml) coconut oil, milk, and salt. Heat over medium heat, stirring constantly, until the mixture begins to bubble and boil. Continue boiling at medium heat, stirring constantly, until mixture reaches 235F (113C) on a candy thermometer (see note), about 5 minutes. The mixture should thicken to the consistency of caramel sundae topping. Remove from heat and stir in the vanilla; pour the mixture over the nuts in the loaf pan.

Allow to cool at room temperature, then place in the refrigerator to cool completely, at least 2 hours.

Once cooled, invert the pan over a cutting board and remove from pan, allowing the slab of caramel to fall to the board; peel away the paper. Cut the caramels into squares as small as you wish.

Make the coating: In a glass or metal bowl set over a pot of simmering water (the bottom of the bowl should not touch the water), melt the chocolate and 2 tsp (10 ml) coconut oil together; stir well. Pour the mixture into a glass measuring cup or small, deep bowl and keep warm.

Using 2 forks to hold the squares steady on either side, dip the caramels into the chocolate. Allow excess chocolate to drip off before placing each caramel on a cooling rack that is positioned over a piece of waxed paper or plastic (to catch any additional drips). Cool at room temperature until the chocolate has set. Store in an airtight container in the refrigerator; bring to room temperature before serving. Makes 12-24 caramels, depending on size.

Note: For years I resisted buying a candy thermometer because something about measuring hot candy scared me. Now I know my fear was unfounded. If you're like I was, you probably don't own a candy thermometer. *You can still make these successfully without one,* but it may take a few tries to get the consistency just right. If the mixture doesn't boil long enough, you'll end up with liquid caramel sauce (in which case you can still make the caramel cup variation, below); if the mixture boils too long, you'll end up with crunchy nut brittle (which, I suppose, you could also coat in chocolate if you wish).

Caramel Cup Variation: Line 12-15 mini muffin cups with foil liners. Spread about 1 tsp (5 ml) of the melted chocolate mixture in each cup, and use the back of a spoon or your finger to coat the bottom and sides evenly. Refrigerate until firm. Then pour 1/2-1 tsp (2.5-5 ml) of the caramel mixture into the cups; refrigerate again until cold. Spoon about 1 tsp of the melted chocolate mixture over top and spread evenly, ensuring that no caramel is left uncovered and that the chocolate seals well at the sides. Refrigerate until solid before removing from the pan. Store covered in an airtight container in the refrigerator; bring to room temperature before serving.

Cocoa Nibbles (LaRaw Bars)

Ridiculously easy, these delicious and satisfying bites provide substantial amounts of calcium and magnesium. And they're so much fresher and less expensive than store-bought raw bars!

1/2 cup (80 g) raw natural almonds (with skin)

1-1/4 cups (150 g) unsweetened dried dates, chopped (they should be soft)

2 Tbsp (30 ml) cocoa powder, preferably not Dutch process

1 tsp (5 ml) pure vanilla extract

Optional add-ins (choose one or two): 6 fresh mint leaves, chopped; 1/4-1/2 tsp (1-2.5 ml) chili flakes; 1 Tbsp (15 ml) chopped candied ginger; 1 Tbsp (15 ml) raw cacao nibs; 2 tsp (10 ml) freshly grated orange zest; 1/2 tsp (2.5 ml) cinnamon; 1-2 tsp (5-10 ml) instant coffee substitute or instant coffee

In the bowl of a food processor, process the almonds, dates and cocoa until you have what looks like a fine meal (there should be no large pieces of almond visible). Sprinkle with the vanilla and any optional add-ins, if using, and continue to process until the mixture comes together in a ball that rolls around the walls of the processor bowl (this may take a while—5 to 10 minutes or so; stop occasionally to scrape the sides of the processor and push the mixture toward the blades).

The "dough" is ready when, if you pinch some and press it between your thumb and fingers, it sticks together readily and appears a bit shiny. (Sometimes, if the dates are too dry, this doesn't happen easily. In that case, sprinkle up to 2 tsp or 5 ml of water along with the vanilla, and proceed as above). The mixture should *not* be as soft as cookie dough, but more like clay in texture.

Place a clean piece of plastic wrap on the counter and turn the mixture onto it. Using your hands, form the mixture into a log about 8 inches (20 cm) long. Try to compress the mixture as much as possible so you have a very dense log. Wrap with plastic and roll the log one or two times, compressing it more with your hands, to squeeze out any air pockets. (Alternately, pat the mixture into an 8" or 20 cm loaf pan; press down as hard as you can to remove any air pockets, then cover with plastic).

If you have a pressing need for chocolate, you can slice and eat the nibbles immediately. However, these are much better if they've been refrigerated first for at least 2 hours or overnight, as they firm up considerably and will attain an almost fudge-like texture when cold. Makes six servings.

Dark and Decadent Chocolate Pâté

With heart-healthy flavonoids from the dark chocolate and monounsaturated fats from the avocado, this is a cholesterol-free indulgence that's actually good for you!

Scant 1/2 cup (115 g) packed avocado purée from a barely ripe avocado (about one small avocado)

1 tsp (5 ml) pure vanilla extract

Pinch fine sea salt

9 ounces (255 g) good quality dark chocolate (70% cocoa is best, but chocolate chips work, too), chopped (about 1-1/2 cups)

1/4 cup (60 ml) freshly squeezed orange juice (remove any large pieces of pulp)

1 Tbsp (15 ml) pure maple syrup

Line a miniature loaf pan (about 6 x 3", or 15 x 7.5 cm) with plastic wrap and set aside.

In the bowl of a food processor, whir the avocado purée, vanilla and salt. Set aside while you melt the chocolate.

In a heavy-bottomed pot set over the lowest heat possible, combine the chocolate, orange juice, and maple syrup. Stir constantly until melted and smooth, about 5 minutes. Immediately scrape the chocolate mixture into the food processor with the avocado, and blend again until perfectly smooth and glossy. Turn the mixture into the loaf pan and smooth the top.

Refrigerate, uncovered, until the top is firm and dry; then cover the top with more plastic wrap and refrigerate until the entire loaf is firm, 4-6 hours or overnight.

To unmold, remove plastic from the top of the loaf. Invert over a serving dish and remove the loaf pan, then carefully peel away the plastic. Serve in thin slices with fresh berries and/or Coconut Whipped "Cream" (page 125). Makes 4-6 servings. May be frozen; defrost, wrapped in plastic, in the refrigerator overnight.

Fruity Cereal Chews

These crisp-and-chewy squares are a great snack or energy bar to take with you when you're out and about. The combination of cereal, fruit and nuts provides sweetness and crunch along with a great array of minerals and protein.

- **3 cups (750 ml) crisped rice or other non-sweet cereal (I use half rice and half unsweetened cornflakes; use rice only for corn-free version)**
- **1/4 cup (35 g) raisins**
- **1/3 cup (45-50 g) chopped nuts (I like cashews and almonds, but it's up to you)**
- **2 Tbsp (30 ml) pumpkin or sunflower seeds**
- **1/3 cup dried cranberries (40 g) or cherries (45 g)**
- **1/4 cup (35 g) chopped dried apricots**
- **1/4 cup (40 g) chopped dried dates**
- **1/2 cup (120 ml) brown rice syrup or barley malt syrup**
- **2 Tbsp (30 ml) blackstrap molasses**
- **2 Tbsp (30 ml) pure maple syrup**
- **3/4 cup (180 ml) natural smooth almond butter**
- **1 tsp (5 ml) pure vanilla extract**
- **1/4 tsp (1 ml) fine sea salt, if almond butter is unsalted**

Preheat oven to 350F (180C). Line a 9" (22.5 cm) square pan with parchment paper, or spray with nonstick spray.

Place the cereal, raisins, nuts, seeds, cranberries, apricots and dates in a large bowl and toss with your hands to mix. Set aside.

Pour the rice syrup, molasses and maple syrup into a small pot and heat over medium heat until mixture bubbles; turn off heat. Add the nut butter and vanilla and stir together quickly. Pour this mixture over the dry ingredients and, working quickly, fold in the wet mixture gently to coat the cereal and other ingredients.

Turn the mixture into prepared pan and press down with your hands firmly to compress it (it's okay if you crunch down some of the cereal at this point) and even the top (it may help to wet your palms slightly). Bake in preheated oven for 10-15 minutes, until the edges are golden and dry. Cool completely before cutting into squares (it helps to refrigerate until firm before cutting; if you cut these while they are still warm, they will fall apart). Makes about 16 squares. Store covered with plastic wrap in the refrigerator for up to one week.

Note: For entirely gluten-free bars, ensure that you use GF rice or corn cereal; many do contain gluten.

Marbled Halvah

When I was a child, one snack that my mom loved was halvah, but I never liked it much. Something must have shifted when I changed my diet, however, because these rich sesame squares are now one of my favorite treats. This version is marbled throughout with a thick ribbon of chocolate, but feel free to leave that out if you're not a fan.

1/2 cup (80 g) cashews, lightly toasted

3/4 cup (180 ml) tahini (sesame paste)

1/4 cup (35 g) sesame seeds, lightly toasted

2 tsp (10 ml) pure vanilla extract

1/3 cup (80 ml) agave nectar, light or dark

1/3 cup (70 g) dairy-free chocolate chips (optional)

In the bowl of a food processor, whir the cashews until they attain the texture of a coarse cornmeal (there should be no pieces larger than sesame seeds). Add the remaining ingredients and process again until the mixture comes together in a homogenous, slightly pasty "dough."

Turn the mixture onto a plastic placemat or cutting board, and push it together to form a disk. Then flatten the disk with your fingers to create a rectangle, about 9 x 8" (22.5 x 20 cm). Set aside.

In a heatproof bowl set over a pan of simmering water (the bowl should sit over the pan without touching the water), melt the chocolate chips. Spread the melted chips evenly over the surface of the rectangle. (Don't worry if the chocolate doesn't cover the entire rectangle or if it begins to firm up as you spread it—the marbling effect is meant to be irregular).

Now, fold the rectangle in thirds, bringing each long edge to the middle (you'll now have a long rectangular "log"). Now fold the short edges toward the middle as well, to create an almost square shape. Fold the square in half again, to create a small rectangular brick.

Flatten the brick slightly to push out any air bubbles and to compact the layers a bit. Wrap tightly in plastic and refrigerate until firm, at least 2-3 hours. Once the halvah is firm, place it on a cutting board and cut into small squares. Store, covered, in the refrigerator. Makes about 20 squares.

Mock Chocolate Pudding

This is one of the first "alternative" desserts I tried after changing my diet. I was thrilled to discover that a substitute for dairy could taste this good, and this close to my memory of the original. The texture of this pudding approximates that of genuine, old-fashioned cooked chocolate pudding, without the cholesterol or high saturated fat.

- **1 package (12 ounces or 375 g) aseptically packaged firm silken Japanese-style tofu (such as Mori-Nu)**
- **1/2 cup (70 g) dark cocoa (preferably not Dutch process)**
- **1/2-1/3 cup (120-160 ml) agave nectar, dark or light (depending on desired level of sweetness)**
- **2 tsp (10 ml) pure vanilla extract**
- **Pinch fine sea salt**

Drain any excess water from the tofu and place it in the bowl of a food processor. Process for about 30 seconds to smooth out the tofu, scraping down the sides of the processor bowl.

In a small, heavy bottomed pot, whisk together the cocoa and agave nectar. Cook, stirring frequently, over medium-low heat just until bubbles begin to form around the edges of the pot. Remove from heat and stir in the vanilla and salt.

Add the cocoa mixture to the processor bowl and blend until completely smooth and velvety, stopping occasionally to scrape down the sides of the bowl (you want to ensure there are no little flecks of tofu visible). The mixture will seem too thin for a pudding at this point; this is as it should be.

Pour into serving dishes. Cover and refrigerate until firm, at least four hours but preferably overnight (this firms up as it chills). Store, covered, in refrigerator for up to 4 days. Makes 4-6 servings.

Raw Fig and Cherry Bars

I originally developed these bars for a cooking class on bone health. Almost every ingredient here is high in calcium, resulting in a bar that delivers about 12% of this mineral's daily requirement for women. They're also high in protein and work as a great energy bar. I often carry these in the car with me for a mid-afternoon pick-me-up.

2 cups (290 g) raw natural almonds (with skin)

1/4 cup (25 g) finely ground flax seeds

Finely grated zest of 2 lemons, preferably organic

1-1/4 cups (190-200 g) quartered dried figs, stems removed (measure after removing stems)

2 Tbsp (30 ml) to 1/4 cup (60 ml) agave nectar, light or dark (to taste and depending on how dry the mixture is)

2 Tbsp (30 ml) raw tahini (sesame paste), or regular, if you're not concerned about the bars being raw

1 cup (120-130 g) dried tart cherries or dried cranberries

Lightly grease a 9″ (22.5 cm) square pan with coconut oil, or line with plastic wrap (I prefer the plastic wrap option).

In the bowl of a large food processor, combine the almonds and flax seeds and process until you have a fine meal that rises up (and begins to cling to) the sides of the bowl (it will appear as if the mixture has stopped spinning except in the very center). Do not overprocess, however, or you'll end up with nut butter!

Add the lemon zest and figs, and process again until well blended and the mixture resembles a coarse meal (there should be no large pieces of fig visible). Add the remaining ingredients and pulse or process briefly to chop the cherries and create a moist dough-like consistency. The mixture is ready if it sticks together and feels slightly moist when pinched between your thumb and fingers.

Turn the mixture into the prepared pan and press down *very* firmly with your fist or the back of a metal spatula (it helps to cover with plastic wrap first). The mixture should be extremely compact and solid—press hard!

Refrigerate until very firm, about an hour, or at least 20 minutes. Cut into 12 bars and store in an airtight container in the refrigerator, or wrap each bar individually in plastic wrap to take along later. The bars will keep, refrigerated, for up to 2 weeks. Makes 12 bars.

Raw Frosted Apricot Raisin Bars

I developed this recipe for a client who had many food restrictions and was following a raw-foods diet. Because the ingredients are all technically "raw," these bars offer a great energy boost in an easily-digestible package. For a fancier version, try them with the coconut-date frosting, as they were enjoyed by my client.

Base:

1 cup (90 g) raw pecan pieces

1/2 cup (70 g) raisins

12-14 dried apricots (they should be very soft), chopped (see note 1)

1 tsp (5 ml) freshly grated orange zest

1/2 cup (40 g) unsweetened shredded coconut

Pinch fine sea salt, if desired

Frosting:

5-1/2 ounces or 150 g (scant 1 cup) dried dates, soaked in room temperature water for 2-3 hours and drained (see note 2)

1/3-1/2 cup (80-120 ml) coconut oil, firm at room temperature, preferably organic (depending on how creamy you want the frosting)

1 Tbsp (15 ml) finely ground chia seeds

1 tsp (5 ml) pure vanilla extract

Reserved date soaking water, as needed

Prepare the base: in the bowl of a food processor, process the pecans briefly to chop. Add raisins, apricots, orange zest, coconut and salt, and process until mixture begins to pull away from sides of bowl (it will look like a dough with crumbs of nut in it). Pinch a bit of the mixture between your thumb and fingers; if it sticks together, it's ready. (If mixture is too dry, you can add water, about a tablespoon or 15 ml at a time, until it holds together).

Pat the mixture firmly into a 9" (22.5 cm) square pan and refrigerate while you make the frosting.

Make the frosting: in a food processor, blend the soaked dates, coconut oil, chia seeds and vanilla until very smooth and no pieces of date are detectable. (You will need to scrape down the sides a few times and add a little of the date soaking water if necessary to get a smooth paste). Spread over base in pan and refrigerate until set, about 3 hours. Cut in small squares. Makes 16-25 servings.

Note 1: if your apricots are a bit dry (versus soft and squishy), soak them in boiling water for 5 minutes (or room temperature water for an hour) and then drain before using in the recipe.

Note 2: Similarly, if you're not concerned about the recipe remaining truly raw, you can soak the dates in boiling water for 5 minutes and then drain (reserving the liquid) before using in the frosting.

Index

Cinnamon

Applesauce Spice Cookies, 72

Banana Bread Pudding and Warm Maple Custard Sauce, 134

Blueberry Coffee Cake, 104

Carrot Raisin Oatmeal Cookies, 75

Carrot Snack Cake, 105

Chai Cheesecake, 138

Chocolate Chip Cookies, 77

Cinnamon Buns, 40

Cinnamon Coffee Toffee Bars, 81

Figaros, 87

Gingered Apple Muffins, 45

Holiday Apple Cake, 119

Maple Millet Muffins, 47

Mini Sweet Potato and Chocolate Chip Muffins, 48

Oatmeal Walnut Scones, 51

Pear and Ginger Mini Loaves or Muffins, 55

Pear Upside Down Cake, 123

Raisin Spice Tea Bread, 59

Spiced Pumpkin and Millet Pudding, 145

Spiced Squash and Cornmeal Muffins, 61

Sunshine Breakfast Loaf, 62

Sweet Harvest Muffins, 63

Sweet Potato and Cranberry Muffins, 64

Tomato Spice Cake, 127

Walnut Cinnamon Rounds, 100

Zucchini and Pineapple Mini Loaves or Muffins, 66

Cloves

Mini Sweet Potato and Chocolate Chip Muffins, 48

Raisin Spice Tea Bread, 59

Rice and Spice Apple Pancakes, 60

Cocoa

Amazing Bean Brownies, 70

Chocolate Layer Cake, 108

Fudgy Chocolate Frosting or Buttercream, 113

Chocolate Ganache Frosting, 107

Chocolate Mint Chocolate Chip Cookies, 78

Chocolate Mystery Cupcakes, 109

Chocolate Peanut Butter Fudgies, 79

Chocolate Satin Tarts, 142

Chocolate Shortbread Cookies, 80

Cocoa Nibbles (LaRaw Bars), 152

Dalmatian Cheesecake Brownies, 84

Gluten-Free, Sugar-Free, Soy-Free Chocolate Buttercream Frosting, 116

Mock Chocolate Pudding, 156

Mrs. K's Date Cake, 122

Ultra Fudgy Brownies, 99

Coconut

Banana Oat Bars, 73

Carrot Snack Cake, 105

Coconut Mini Loaves or Cupcakes, 112

Coconut Macaroons, 83

Ginger Coconut Cookies, 88

Mrs. K's Date Cake, 122

Pecan Coconut Chews—Baked or Raw!, 93

Raw Frosted Apricot Raisin Bars, 158

Tropical Lemon Coconut Muffins, 65

Coconut Milk

Banana Bread Pudding and Warm Maple Custard Sauce, 134

Berries and Cream Tart, 135

Chai Cheesecake, 138

Chocolate Satin Tarts, 142

Gluten-Free, Sugar-Free, Soy-Free Pastry Cream, 117

Gluten-Free, Soy-Free Chocolate Buttercream Frosting, 116

Soy Free, Sugar Free Coconut Whipped Cream, 125

Soy Free, Sugar Free Coconut Whipped Cream, 125

Spiced Pumpkin Millet Pudding, 145

Coconut Oil

Butter Tarts, 136

Berries and Cream Tart, 135

Cashew Chocolate Chip Cookies, 76

Cinnamon Buns, 40

Chocolate Caramels, 150

Fudgy Chocolate Frosting or Buttercream, 113

Chocolate Pecan Pie, 140

Chocolate Shortbread Cookies, 80

Chocolate Satin Tarts, 142

Coconut Mini Loaves or Cupcakes, 112

Ginger Coconut Cookies, 88

Glazed Almond Bars, 89

Light Lemony Buttercream Frosting, 120

Gluten-Free, Sugar-Free, Soy-Free Chocolate Buttercream Frosting, 116

Hazelnut Mocha Cookies, 90

Raisin Spice Tea Bread, 59

Crêpes
Corn Crêpes, 42

Cupcakes
Coconut Mini Loaves or Cupcakes, 112

Dates or Date Purée
Carob and Date Pancakes, 38

Cashew "Cream," 106

Cashew Date Bread, 39

Chocolate Chip Cookies, 77

Chocolate Mint Chocolate Chip Cookies, 78

Cinnamon Walnut Coffee Cake, 110

Cocoa Nibbles (LaRaw Bars), 152

Dalmatian Cheesecake Brownies, 84

Fruity Cereal Chews, 154

Maple Millet Muffins, 47

Mrs. K's Date Cake, 122

Multi-Seed Muffins, 49

Orange Oat Muffins, 52

PB & G Muffins, 54

Pecan Coconut Chews—Baked or Raw!, 93

Raw Frosted Apricot Raisin Bars, 158

Zucchini and Pineapple Mini Loaves or Muffins, 66

Eggplant
Chocolate Peanut Butter Fudgies, 79

Figs
Figaros, 87

Raw Fig and Cherry Bars, 157

Frostings, Toppings, Fillings
Cashew Cream, 106

Gluten-Free, Sugar-Free, Soy-Free Chocolate Buttercream Frosting, 116

Chocolate Ganache Frosting, 107

Fudgy Chocolate Frosting or Buttercream, 113

Gluten-Free, Sugar-Free, Soy-Free Chocolate Buttercream Frosting, 116

Light Lemony Buttercream Frosting, 120

Gluten-Free, Sugar-Free, Soy-Free Pastry Cream, 117

Raw Date-Coconut Frosting (from Raw Frosted Apricot Raisin Bars), 158

Soy Free, Sugar Free Coconut Whipped Cream, 125

Vanilla Pastry Cream or Buttercream Frosting, 128

Garbanzo Bean (Chickpea) Flour (Besan)
Coconut Mini Loaves or Cupcakes, 112

Ginger
Carrot Snack Cake, 105

Chai Cheesecake, 138

Gingered Apple Muffins, 45

Ginger Coconut Cookies, 88

Mini Sweet Potato and Chocolate Chip Muffins, 48

Pear and Ginger Mini Loaves or Muffins, 55

PB & G Muffins, 54

Pecan Coconut Chews—Baked or Raw!, 93

Rice and Spice Apple Pancakes, 60

Spiced Pumpkin and Millet Pudding, 145

Spiced Squash and Cornmeal Muffins, 61

Sweet Harvest Muffins, 63

Tomato Spice Cake, 127

Twice Spiced Ginger Cookies, 98

Grapefruit Juice or Zest
Figaros, 87

Hazelnuts
Hazelnut Mocha Cookies, 90

Lemon Flavor, Juice or Zest
Blueberry Coffee Cake, 104

Carrot Snack Cake, 105

Chai Cheesecake, 138

Glazed Lemon Poppyseed Bundt Cake, 115

Light Lemony Buttercream Frosting, 120

Lemon Blueberry Scones, 46

My Mother's Cheesecake, 143

Pear Upside Down Cake, 123

Raw Fig and Cherry Bars, 157

Tropical Lemon Coconut Muffins, 65

Loaves and Breads
Banana Chocolate Chip Mini Loaves or Muffins, 36

Cashew Date Bread, 39

Cinnamon Buns, 40

Pear and Ginger Mini Loaves or Muffins, 55

Poppyseed Soda Bread, 58

Raisin Spice Tea Bread, 59

Sunshine Breakfast Loaf, 62

Zucchini and Pineapple Mini Loaves or Muffins, 66

Macadamia Nut Butter
Coconut Mini Loaves or Cupcakes, 112

Macadamia Sesame Cookies, 91

Nutmeg

Banana Bread Pudding and Warm Maple Custard Sauce, 134

Maple Millet Muffins, 47

Mini Sweet Potato and Chocolate Chip Muffins, 48

Raisin Spice Tea Bread, 59

Spiced Pumpkin and Millet Pudding, 145

Sweet Potato and Cranberry Muffins, 64

Nuts or Nut Butters (see also individual types of nut)

Almond Butter Spice Cookies, 71

Banana Nut Muffins, 37

Blueberry Coffee Cake, 104

Cashew Cream, 106

Cashew Date Bread, 39

Chai Cheesecake, 138 (crust only)

Chocolate Caramels, 150

Chocolate Pecan Pie, 140

Chocolate Peanut Butter Fudgies, 79

Cinnamon Coffee Toffee Bars, 81

Cinnamon Walnut Coffee Cake, 110

Classic Peanut Butter Cookies, 82

Coconut Mini Loaves or Cupcakes, 112

Dalmatian Cheesecake Brownies, 84

Fruity Cereal Chews, 154

Glazed Almond Bars, 89

Maple Walnut Cookies, 92

Marbled Halvah, 155

Macadamia Sesame Cookies, 91

Multi-Seed Muffins, 49

My Mother's Cheesecake, 143 Oatmeal Walnut Scones, 51

Orange Pistachio Scones, 46

Pear and Ginger Mini Loaves or Muffins, 55

Pear and Pecan Scones, 56

Pear Upside Down Cake, 123

Pecan Coconut Chews—Baked or Raw!, 93

Raw Fig and Cherry Bars, 157

Raw Frosted Apricot Raisin Bars, 158

Seed Jumble Cookies, 95

Spiced Pumpkin and Millet Pudding 145

Sunshine Breakfast Loaf, 62

Triple C Cookies, 97

Walnut Cinnamon Rounds, 100

Oat Bran

Oatbran Banana Muffins, 50

Oat Flour

Applesauce Spice Cookies, 72

Banana Oat Bars, 73

Chocolate Mystery Cupcakes, 109

Macadamia Sesame Cookies, 91

PB & G Muffins, 54

Pear and Ginger Mini-Loaves or Muffins, 55

Dalmatian Cheesecake Brownies, 84

Sweet Harvest Muffins, 63

Tropical Lemon Coconut Muffins, 65

Oats, whole

Applesauce Spice Cookies, 72

Almond Butter Spice Cookies, 71

Banana Oat Bars, 73

Blueberry Coffee Cake, 104

Carrot Raisin Oatmeal Cookies, 75

Chai Cheesecake, 138

Cinnamon Walnut Coffee Cake, 110

French Toast Soufflé with Summer Berries, 44

Oatmeal-Walnut Scones, 51

Orange Oat Muffins, 52

Plum Good Oaty Pancakes, 57

Seed Jumble Cookies, 95

Orange (whole)

Orange Oat Muffins, 52

Orange Juice or Zest

Chocolate Layer Cake, 108

Cinnamon Buns, 40

Dark and Decadent Chocolate Pâté, 153

Figaros, 87

Orange Pistachio Scones, 46

Orange Raisin Tea Cakes, 53

Pecan Coconut Chews—Baked or Raw!, 93

Plum-Topped Cornmeal Cake, 124

Raw Frosted Apricot Raisin Bars, 158

Sunshine Breakfast Loaf, 62

Sweet Potato and Cranberry Muffins, 64

Twice Spiced Ginger Cookies, 98

Pancakes

Carob and Date Pancakes, 38

Corn Crêpes, 42

Fluffy Fruited Pancakes, 43

Plum Good Oaty Pancakes, 57

Rice and Spice Apple Pancakes, 60

Scones, Biscuits and Buns

Cinnamon Buns, 40

Classic Cranberry Scones 46

Lemon Blueberry Scones, 46

Oatmeal Walnut Scones, 51

Orange Pistachio Scones, 46

Orange Raisin Tea Cakes, 53

Pear and Pecan Scones, 56

Sesame Seeds (see also Tahini)

Macadamia Sesame Cookies, 91

Marbled Halvah, 155

Multi-Seed Muffins, 49

Seed Jumble Cookies, 95

Sorghum Flour

Amazing Bean Brownies, 70

Coconut Mini Loaves or Cupcakes, 112

Soufflé

French Toast Soufflé with Summer Berries, 44

Spinach

Chocolate Mystery Cupcakes, 109

Sweet Harvest Muffins, 63

Squash

Spiced Squash and Cornmeal Muffins, 61

Sunflower Seeds

Fruity Cereal Chews, 154

Multi-Seed Muffins, 49

Seed Jumble Cookies, 95

Sweet Potato

Mini Sweet Potato and Chocolate Chip Muffins, 48

Sweet Potato-Cranberry Muffins 64

Tahini (Sesame Seed Paste)

Amazing Bean Brownies, 70

Cashew Chocolate Chip Cookies, 76

Cashew Date Bread, 39

Macadamia Sesame Cookies, 91

Coconut Macaroons, 83

Maple Walnut Cookies, 92

Marbled Halvah, 155

Raw Fig and Cherry Bars, 157

Seed Jumble Cookies, 95

Tarts (see Pies and Tarts)

Tea

Raisin Spice Tea Bread, 59

Tofu

Almond Butter Spice Cookies, 71

Dalmatian Cheesecake Brownies, 84

Gingered Apple Muffins, 45

Mock Chocolate Pudding, 156

My Mother's Cheesecake, 143

Pear Upside Down Cake, 123

Tomato

Tomato Spice Cake, 127

Walnuts

Blueberry Coffee Cake, 104

Cinnamon Walnut Coffee Cake, 110

Chai Cheesecake, 138

Chocolate Caramels, 150

Maple Walnut Cookies, 92

Oatmeal Walnut Scones, 51

Pear and Ginger Mini Loaves or Muffins, 55

Pear Upside Down Cake, 123

Sunshine Breakfast Loaf, 62

Walnut Cinnamon Rounds, 100

Xanthan Gum

Coconut Mini Loaves or Cupcakes, 112

Zucchini

Chocolate Mystery Cupcakes, 109

Sweet Harvest Muffins, 63

Zucchini and Pineapple Mini Loaves or Muffins, 66